LAKE RABUN
Dockside Delights

COOKING

THE LAKE RABUN

WAY

LAKE RABUN
DOCKSIDE DELIGHTS

COOKING
THE LAKE RABUN
WAY

Published by Lake Rabun Food and Fun, Inc.
Copyright © 2003 by
Lake Rabun Food and Fun, Inc.
1485 Rucker Circle
Woodstock, Georgia 30188
(770) 442-9065

ISBN 0-9727165-0-5

Edited, Designed, and Manufactured by

CommunityClassics™
an imprint of

FRP™

P.O. Box 305142
Nashville, Tennessee 37230
(800) 358-0560

Cover Art: Libby Mathews
Photographer: Bruce Schnaak

Manufactured in the United States of America
First Printing: 2003
5,000 copies

All proceeds shall benefit the Lake Rabun Foundation
and various community projects.

COOKBOOK COMMITTEE

Betsy Bairstow Morse
Nancy Pruitt
Co-Chairmen

Carol Raeber
Section Chairman

Ann Webb
Art Chairman

Jean Sheldon
Treasurer

Michele Sharpton
Donna Kay Deas
Jill Dyas
Co-Chairmen
Tasting Parties

Billy McKinnon
Recipe Advisor

Becky Jackson
Recipe Coordinator

Mary Cobb Stone
History Chairman

Barbara Persons Roper
History

Donna Kay Deas
Pre-Sales Chairman

Yetty Arp
Barrie Aycock
Pat Clay
Gail Davenport
Mary Evans
Mary V. Grigsby
Jo Ann Lampe
Roses Longino
Dana Halberg Pless

Without the vision and dedication of Betsy Bairstow Morse,
this cookbook would never have become a reality.

Thank you, Betsy!

ABOUT THE ARTIST

LIBBY MATHEWS

Libby Mathews' early experience was filled with years of printmaking, teaching with the Fulton Council for the Arts and the Georgia Arts Council, and dancing with the Mary Staton Dance Ensemble. Once she began painting, however, nothing else held her interest quite as strongly. She created her own course of study with painters whose work she most admired. Marc Chatov and his uncle, Roman, were her first instructors. Artist Alice Edgar Williams took her outside to paint "en plein air" and the spark ignited. Libby's Gestalt love of landscape has taken her to Wyoming, California, Central America, and Italy to paint. The time she spent as a Hambidge Fellow in Rabun Gap gave her a dynamic focus that has grown with time.

ABOUT THE PHOTOGRAPHER

BRUCE SCHNAAK

Bruce worked in the commercial photography business in Atlanta prior to moving to Lake Rabun ten years ago. He is still active in various photo and graphic design projects involving people, landscapes, and product work. But you may know him as one of the "B's" in B&B Painting.

TABLE OF CONTENTS

DEDICATION   6

INTRODUCTION   7

ABOUT THE BOATHOUSES   10

APPETIZERS AND BEVERAGES   12

SOUPS AND SALADS   32

MEAT AND PASTA DISHES   62

POULTRY AND SEAFOOD   82

SIDE DISHES   104

BREADS AND BREAKFAST   138

DESSERTS   164

RESTAURANT RECIPE CONTRIBUTORS   204

CONTRIBUTORS   205

INDEX   208

ORDER INFORMATION   215

DEDICATION

HERTA ANDREAE SCHARTLE

Herta was born in Rabun County
before Rabun's Mathis Dam was built.
She lived the history of Rabun County
as the lakes were impounded and the
Tallulah Falls Railway flourished. She
witnessed the growing influx of summer
visitors and was an integral part in the
establishment of the Lake Rabun Hotel.
Her charm, grace, and love have
made her the true "Lady of the Lake."

With much love and deep appreciation,
we dedicate this book to Herta
for the lake she so loves.

INTRODUCTION

Lake Rabun, or "Lakemont," is a jewel nestled in the majestic Blue Ridge Mountains in the northeast corner of Georgia. The towering green pine and hemlock trees grow to the water's edge and are laced with mountain laurel, rhododendron, and wild azaleas. The dark green shimmering waters reflect this splendor of nature. The romantic tales and lore of early days have made the history and beauty of this lake a treasure for nearly a century.

By 1905, the Tallulah Falls Railroad had completed its route from Cornelia, Georgia, to Lakemont, Georgia, a small town only a few miles from the site of Lake Rabun today. In this era, most travel had been by horse and wagon. The new railroad brought the ability to tap this region's resources for industry and recreation.

In the early 1900s, the Georgia Railway and Power Company decided to build a series of lakes to generate hydroelectric power to serve Atlanta and other north Georgia towns. Lake Rabun was the first of four lakes built in stair-step elevations with Lake Burton being the highest in elevation. The source of water was the Tallulah River, which ran through this valley.

Tallulah Gorge in nearby Tallulah Falls was already a booming attraction to visitors and a favorite destination of honeymooners. Many hotels were built along the new railway near the edge of the gorge. Some of the memorable hotels were Glen Brook Hotel, Tallulah Lodge, Cliff House, Robinson Hotel, and Willard House.

Unfortunately, in 1921, most of the town's magnificent hotels and inns were destroyed in a devastating fire at Christmas time when blustery winds spread the flames to the homes, stores, and hotels. In Lakemont, the Lakemont Lodge and Crows Nest were not in danger.

The dam impounding Lake Rabun was completed in 1915, but the first settlers had discovered the area years earlier. Augustus Andreae, a German immigrant, was the most noted. He came to the area to raise silkworms for the silk industry, but when his venture failed, he began buying land in the valley and along the Tallulah River. Later he exchanged with Georgia Railway and Power Company much of his valley property for land along the shore of the new lake that was being built. Most of the first lake properties were sold by Mr. Andreae. He acquired the Lake Rabun Hotel soon after it was built, and his family ran it for many years. His two daughters, Herta Schartle and Rita Collins, grew up at the hotel and have remained an integral part of the lake community through the years.

Some of the first summer homes built on Lake Rabun were the families of Preston Arkright, William Prescott, Andrew Hansell, Stuart Witham, Samuel and Candler Dobbs, Lindsay Hopkins, Sr., Dr. George H. Bellinger, F.O. Stone, Winship Nunnally, Sr., J.O. King, Sr., Clarence Ruse, Candler Guy, and James R. Gray. There were nearly twenty families making Lake Rabun their summer residence by the end of the 1920s.

Haslett's Store (now Lake House Antiques) opened in 1922 across from the Lake Rabun Hotel. It provided necessities like flour, chickens, eggs, and ice. Most produce was brought up on the Tallulah Falls Railway and then transported to the lake by Model T Hack. According to Mr. Haslett, if the load was too heavy coming over the mountain, often the crates of chickens were off loaded and left by the side of the road because the ice was melting and had to be delivered quickly. The chickens were picked up on a second trip. In later years, Noah Beck lived in that location and sold fresh milk from his cow to the lake residents.

Alley's Store in Lakemont, across from the Lakemont Train Depot, was also a necessary stop for provisions of all kinds—hardware, ice, and even worms for fishing. Alley's housed the Lakemont Post Office where Mrs. Alley served as its postmistress. Alley's also had one of the first telephones. Alley's is still owned by the original family and is operated by Lamar Alley.

In the 1930s, the number of lake homeowners grew and the Wilcoxon, Raine, Ellis, Gay, and Doonan families now called Lakemont their summer home. Transportation to the lake was still an all-day affair—mostly on dirt or gravel roads, which were almost impassible during heavy rains. Sometimes an overnight stay in Cornelia was necessary. Often a block of ice would be strapped to the front bumper of the car to be used as refrigeration for perishable foods. Most homes did not have refrigerators or electricity, and no one had a telephone.

Mass production of cars and paved roads opened access to the lake to many more families in the 1940s and 1950s, including the Dyases, Branches, Waltons, and Bondurants. Even though most roads were only two-lane highways, the trip from Atlanta was now only three or four hours instead of all day. Some families like the Longinos, Jones, and Pruitts came for the entire summer and organized activities were planned for the children—summer school at the lake.

The 1950s and 1960s saw more boating activity on the lake. Fishing and aquaplaning gave way to water skiing—mostly behind boats with small outboard motors.

From the 1960s through the 1990s, more new homes were built and more families discovered "Shangrila"—Fred Stewart's description of Lake Rabun. Movie producers also discovered the area. *The Great Locomotive Chase*, *Deliverance*, and *Decorations Day* were filmed on the lake and nearby. Sightings of movie stars like Burt Reynolds or James Garner caused quite a stir of excitement on the lake.

Lake Rabun has entered the 21st century with all the cherished memories of the early days and the traditions handed down from earlier generations. Lake Rabun, or "Lakemont," will always be a special place where families will come to share good times and experience the unique blend of past and present. This book represents some of the many special foods shared at these family gatherings over the years. Enjoy these *Dockside Delights*.

ABOUT THE BOATHOUSES

WITHAM

This boathouse has been in the Witham family for four generations. It was built by Cyrill Smith, an English architect, who built five manor houses in the United States and then retired. One of the most notable features of this boathouse is the bright red geraniums that fill the planters on all sides of the structure.

GUY

This is one of the oldest boathouses on the lake and was purchased by the Guys in 1936. It was constructed primarily as a place for parties and the interior features a large bar. The significant architectural feature is the cupola, a perfect spot to sit on the big swing and look at the lake.

MATHEWS

Built in 1938, this boathouse has the original oak diving board that still has bounce and gives pleasure to all who dare to walk the plank. The boathouse has remained loyal to the original "Lakemont" green with white trim. In 1992, the single-stall boathouse had a shed boat slip added as well as a dock and dock extensions. The 1952 wooden Chris-Craft is housed very happily in her vintage boathouse.

Built in 2001 and made primarily of cedar shake, locust logs, and twigs, this boathouse was designed to reflect the character of the lake and blend with the natural beauty of the lakefront. Positioned at the mouth of the narrows, the boathouse provides a beautiful sunrise view overlooking the Big Basin.

HOLMES-SHLESINGER

This boathouse, named "TH' OTHER PLACE," was built in 1975 for the Wrigley family as a lake cottage. It has an open porch with keeping room, two bedrooms plus a dorm room. The porch has a beautiful view of the mountains at cocktail hour when Chris- Crafts go cruising by. Late in the evening, you can hear the waterfall across the lake.

WRIGLEY

The Chalet has been a landmark on the lake for over 70 years. First constructed by William Bellinger in the late 1920s, this replica of a Swiss Alps Chalet has withstood the test of time. The Clay family has owned it for over fifty years. Newly restored, the Chalet is available for weekly rentals year-round.

CHALET

Designed by Bob and Belle Voyles who sketched their plans on a piece of paper and shared them with Atlanta designer William Baker, this "Camp Lakemont" boathouse reflects early 1920s Lake Rabun architecture and detail that was updated to provide for the active lifestyle of the Voyles' four teenage children.

VOYLES

From Pinball Machines To No Dancing On Sundays

The marina on Lake Rabun has always been the gathering place and has seen many changes through the years. It was originally called Patterson's, then Harvey's, and later (there were two competing ownerships) Hall's Boathouse and Rabun Boathouse. Hall's was owned and operated by Guy Hall and was known for its "icy co-colas" and pinball machines. The attendants who pumped gas wore khaki or white uniforms with their names embroidered on their shirts. Hall's Boathouse also had a long row of built-in benches where anyone could sit, feed the fish, and watch boats come and go. There was a memorable big sign on the wall that said "No Dancing On Sundays." Across the small cove was Rabun Boathouse, which was owned and operated by Fred Worley, who could be recognized by the captain's hat he always wore. Rabun Boathouse was noted for its "rock 'n' roll" jukebox, bowling alley machine, and dancing on Saturday nights on its large covered dock. Hall's and Rabun Boathouses both offered, for a small fee, tours of the lake in their big wooden Chris-Craft boats. The only surviving boat from this fleet is "Hall's Boathouse No. 1," which has been restored and now resides on Lake Rabun. These two boathouses are now gone and have been replaced by a new facility called Lakemont Marine, Inc., which services the lake residents.

APPETIZERS AND BEVERAGES

Scallops in Scotch and Cream

1¹/₄ pounds scallops
Salt and pepper to taste
³/₄ cup Scotch whisky
2 cups whipping cream

Combine the scallops, salt, pepper and whisky in a skillet and mix
well. Cook over high heat for 2 to 3 minutes or just until the scallops
are firm, stirring frequently. Drain the scallops, reserving the liquid in
a saucepan. Place the scallops on a plate; cover loosely to keep warm.
Cook the reserved liquid over high heat until reduced by ²/₃, stirring
frequently and adding any liquid accumulated on the plate of scallops.
Stir in 1¹/₂ cups of the cream. Reduce to ³/₄ cup, stirring frequently.
Remove from the heat. Add the scallops. Beat the remaining cream in a
mixing bowl until soft peaks form. Fold into the scallop mixture. Spoon
into a baking dish. Broil for 30 seconds to glaze the surface of the sauce.
Garnish with a sprig of curly-leaf parsley. **Yield: 4 servings.**

*Note: You may serve the scallops in ramekins or a chafing dish as a first course.
Serve with wooden picks or cocktail forks. This is delicious. The sauce reductions
are very important.*

14

BACON CHEESE SQUARES

1 cup mayonnaise
1/2 cup (2 ounces) shredded
    sharp Cheddar cheese

1 tablespoon sherry
1/2 cup real bacon bits
30 Triscuits

Combine the mayonnaise, cheese, sherry and bacon in a bowl and mix well. Spread 1 tablespoon of the mixture over each cracker. Arrange on a baking sheet. Broil for 1 to 2 minutes or until the mixture is bubbly; do not burn. **Yield: 30 squares.**

Note: These squares are always popular. The ingredients are easy to have on hand for last-minute appetizers.

CREAM CHEESE ROLL-UPS

16 ounces cream cheese, softened
1 envelope ranch salad
    dressing mix
4 green onions, chopped
1 (4-ounce) can green chiles,
    drained

1 (4-ounce) jar diced pimentos,
    drained
1/3 cup chopped black olives
6 (8-inch) flour tortillas

Beat the cream cheese and dressing mix in a mixing bowl until fluffy. Stir in the green onions, green chiles, pimentos and black olives. Spread equal portions of the mixture over each tortilla. Roll up each tortilla. Wrap with plastic wrap. Chill for 3 hours or up to 1 week. Cut each roll-up into 10 slices. Arrange on a serving plate. **Yield: 5 dozen roll-ups.**

MUSHROOM SQUARES

1 (4-ounce) can mushroom pieces
    and stems, drained and
    chopped
2 slices bacon, crisp-cooked and
    crumbled
2 tablespoons shredded Swiss
    cheese

2 tablespoons mayonnaise
1 tablespoon parsley
1/8 teaspoon rosemary leaves,
    crumbled
Pinch of salt
6 slices white bread
Butter, softened

Combine the mushrooms, bacon, cheese, mayonnaise, parsley, rosemary and salt in a bowl and mix well. Trim and discard the crusts from the bread. Spread the bread with butter. Cut each slice into 4 squares. Arrange buttered side down on a baking sheet. Spoon a small amount of the mushroom mixture onto each square. Bake at 400 degrees for 5 minutes. Serve immediately. **Yield: 24 squares.**

OLIVE CAPER CROSTINI

1/2 cup Greek olives, pitted
3 tablespoons extra-virgin olive oil
1 tablespoon chopped fresh basil
1 tablespoon capers

2 garlic cloves
1 baguette, cut into 1/2-inch slices
1/2 cup olive oil or melted unsalted
    butter

Combine the olives, 3 tablespoons olive oil, basil, capers and garlic in a food processor. Process until puréed. Arrange the baguette slices on a baking sheet. Brush with 1/2 cup olive oil. Bake at 400 degrees for 8 to 10 minutes or until crisp and brown. Let stand to cool. Spread with the olive mixture and serve. **Yield: 48 crostini.**

Note: This appetizer is an Italian treat!

Pears on Pumpernickel

5 ripe pears
1½ tablespoons lemon juice
3 teaspoons honey mustard
1 package cocktail pumpernickel
　　bread

16 ounces Monterey Jack cheese,
　　thinly sliced

Peel the pears and cut into thin slices. Brush with the lemon juice to prevent browning. Spread a small amount of the honey mustard over each bread slice. Arrange on a baking sheet. Top with a cheese slice and a few pear slices. Bake at 400 degrees for 5 minutes or until the cheese is bubbly. **Yield: 24 appetizers.**

Note: These appetizers look and taste great served with red and green grapes and are especially good paired with wine.

Lake Rabun Salmon Bites

½ smoked salmon, coarsely
　　chopped
1 medium red onion, finely
　　chopped
2 tablespoons capers

2 tablespoons lemon juice
3 tablespoons finely chopped
　　fresh chives
1 baguette, thinly sliced
½ cup garlic olive oil

Combine the salmon, onion, capers, lemon juice and chives in a bowl and mix well. Toast the baguette slices lightly. Brush with the olive oil. Spoon 1 teaspoon of the salmon mixture onto each piece of toast. Serve on a platter garnished with caperberries, chopped kalamata olives and lemon slices. **Yield: 24 bites.**

Note: This is a beautiful dish and always a hit.

TOMATO BASIL BRUSCHETTA

2 ripe red tomatoes
2 ripe yellow tomatoes
1/4 cup chopped red onion
1/4 cup extra-virgin olive oil
1/4 cup balsamic vinegar

2 tablespoons chopped fresh basil
2 teaspoons salt
1 teaspoon pepper
1 baguette, cut into 1/4-inch slices

Chop the tomatoes, discarding the seeds. Combine the tomatoes, onion, olive oil, balsamic vinegar, basil, salt and pepper in a bowl and mix well. Let stand for 30 minutes. Spread the tomato mixture over the baguette slices. **Yield: 24 bruschetta.**

Note: You may drizzle the baguette slices with olive oil and toast at 450 degrees until crisp before spreading the slices with the tomato mixture.

FRIED GREEN TOMATO SANDWICHES

1 box WhistleStop Batter Mix
3 green tomatoes, sliced
Mayonnaise
12 slices good-quality white bread,
    toasted

12 slices bacon, crisp-cooked
6 slices mozzarella cheese

Prepare the batter mix using the package directions. Coat the green tomatoes with the batter and fry using the package directions. Spread a small amount of mayonnaise over half the bread slices. Top with the fried green tomatoes, bacon, cheese and remaining bread slices. Cut into quarters. Serve immediately. **Yield: 6 servings.**

Turkey Mozzarella Rabun Picnic Sandwiches

1 (1¹/₂-pound) round sourdough bread
¹/₃ cup zesty Italian salad dressing
6 to 8 spinach leaves, stems removed
1 cup (4 ounces) shredded mozzarella cheese
1 small red onion, thinly sliced
6 to 8 thin slices deli turkey breast
1 small tomato, thinly sliced
¹/₂ cucumber, peeled and thinly sliced

Cut and reserve a slice from the top of the bread. Remove and discard the center of the bread, leaving a ¹/₂-inch shell. Brush the inside of the shell and top with the salad dressing. Layer the spinach, half the cheese, onion, turkey, tomato, cucumber and remaining cheese in the shell. Replace the top of the bread. Wrap in foil. Bake at 350 degrees for 45 minutes. Let stand to cool for 10 minutes. Cut into wedges. Serve warm or cold. **Yield: 6 servings.**

Famous Grilled PBJs

Peanut butter
8 slices favorite bread
Jelly
½ cup (1 stick) butter or margarine, softened

Spread peanut butter over 4 of the bread slices. Spread with jelly. Top with the remaining bread slices. Spread the butter over both sides of the sandwiches. Grill in a skillet until golden brown, turning once. **Yield: 4 sandwiches.**

Note: These sandwiches bring out the kid in all of us.

Poppy Cheese Sticks

1 loaf thinly sliced bread (white preferred)
8 ounces grated Parmesan cheese
2 tablespoons poppy seeds
1 teaspoon celery salt
1 teaspoon paprika
2 cups (4 sticks) corn oil margarine, melted

Trim and discard the crusts from the bread. Cut each bread slice into 3 strips. Combine the cheese, poppy seeds, celery salt and paprika in a shallow dish and mix well. Brush both sides of the bread with the butter. Coat with the cheese mixture. Arrange on a lightly greased baking sheet. Bake at 325 degrees for 15 to 20 minutes or until crisp and brown. Remove to paper towels to cool. **Yield: 24 to 30 breadsticks.**

Note: Kids love these breadsticks.

HARVEST BRIE

1 (15-ounce) round Brie cheese
1 unbaked (9-inch) deep-dish pie shell
1 (21-ounce) can apple pie filling
1 to 2 tablespoons butter or margarine, cut into small pieces (optional)

Place the cheese in the center of the pie shell. Pour the pie filling over and around the cheese, topping the cheese with a few apple slices. Dot with the butter. Bake at 425 degrees for 30 minutes or until the pie shell is golden brown and the cheese is heated through but not melted. Let stand for 10 minutes. Serve with crackers. **Yield: 20 servings.**

Note: You may add 1 tablespoon whisky or brandy or 1/4 cup chopped nuts. Cut through the crust to serve. Reduce the oven temperature to 375 degrees if baking in a glass dish.

CHÈVRE WITH SUN-DRIED TOMATOES AND BASIL

Olive oil
8 ounces chèvre
4 ounces oil-pack sun-dried tomatoes, drained and chopped
1/2 teaspoon minced garlic
1/2 cup chopped fresh basil

Coat a baking dish with olive oil. Place the cheese in the prepared baking dish. Bake at 400 degrees for 15 to 20 minutes or until melted. Combine the sun-dried tomatoes, garlic and basil in a bowl and mix well. Spoon over the cheese. Serve with crackers or fresh vegetables. **Yield: 12 servings.**

Note: Guests love this spread.

PEPPERED MARINATED GOAT CHEESE

1/3 cup loosely packed sun-dried
    tomatoes, chopped
24 green peppercorns
Freshly ground black pepper
3 garlic cloves

1/2 cup fresh basil, chopped
1/2 cup fresh oregano, chopped
Extra-virgin olive oil
1 (10- to 11-ounce) log goat
    cheese, cut into 9 slices

Combine the sun-dried tomatoes with enough water to cover in a small microwave-safe bowl. Microwave, tightly covered with plastic wrap, on High for 5 minutes. Drain and place on paper towels to remove the moisture. Layer 8 green peppercorns, a pinch of black pepper, 1 garlic clove, 2 1/2 teaspoons basil, 2 1/2 teaspoons oregano and 2 teaspoons sun-dried tomatoes in each of three 1/2-pint jars. Fill jars halfway with olive oil and mix well. Place a cheese slice in each jar. Layer the remaining basil, oregano, sun-dried tomatoes and cheese in each jar to make 3 layers. Fill the jars with olive oil, leaving 1/2 inch headspace. Marinate, covered, for 2 days in the refrigerator before serving. Use within 2 to 3 weeks for best flavor. Serve at room temperature. **Yield: 3 (1/2-pint) jars.**

HEARTS OF PALM SPREAD

1 (14-ounce) can hearts of palm,
    drained and chopped
1 cup (4 ounces) shredded
    mozzarella cheese
1/2 cup grated Parmesan cheese

3/4 cup light mayonnaise
1/4 cup sour cream
2 tablespoons minced green onions
Paprika to taste

Combine the hearts of palm, mozzarella cheese, Parmesan cheese, mayonnaise, sour cream and green onions in a bowl and mix well. Spoon into a greased 9-inch quiche pan or pie plate. Sprinkle with paprika. Bake at 350 degrees for 20 minutes or until bubbly and brown. Serve with crackers. **Yield: 24 servings.**

HERBED CHEESECAKE

1 cup butter cracker crumbs
3 tablespoons butter, melted
16 ounces cream cheese, softened
1 cup sour cream
6 ounces crumbled goat cheese

3 eggs
1/4 cup chopped fresh chives
2 tablespoons minced fresh thyme
1 cup sour cream
Spinach leaves

Combine the cracker crumbs and butter in a bowl and mix well. Press onto the bottom of an 8-inch springform pan. Combine the cream cheese, 1 cup sour cream and goat cheese in a mixing bowl. Beat at medium speed until smooth. Add the eggs 1 at a time, beating well after each addition. Stir in the chives and thyme. Spoon into the prepared pan. Bake at 325 degrees for 40 minutes. Let stand to cool. Chill, covered, for 8 hours or freeze for up to 1 month. Spread 1 cup sour cream over the top. Remove the side of the pan. Place on a bed of spinach leaves on a serving plate. Serve with assorted crackers. **Yield: 8 to 10 servings.**

SEAFOOD PIZZA

8 ounces cream cheese, softened
Pinch of garlic powder
1 tablespoon mayonnaise
Dash of Worcestershire sauce
1 (12-ounce) bottle cocktail sauce
1 can lump crab meat, drained
    and flaked
1 can shrimp, drained

1 cup (4 ounces) shredded
    mozzarella cheese
1 cup (4 ounces) shredded
    Monterey Jack cheese
1 small can black olives, sliced
1 bunch green onions, chopped
1 small green bell pepper, chopped

Mix the first 4 ingredients in a bowl. Spread on a round dish to resemble a pizza crust. Spread with cocktail sauce, leaving a 1/2-inch rim. Sprinkle evenly with the crab meat and shrimp. Sprinkle with the mozzarella cheese, Monterey Jack cheese, black olives, green onions and bell pepper. Serve with crackers. **Yield: 24 servings.**

BLT Dip

6 slices bacon, crisp-cooked and crumbled
1 cup sour cream
1 cup mayonnaise
4 plum tomatoes, seeded and chopped (about 1 cup)
3 tablespoons chopped fresh parsley
1/4 cup (or more) chopped lettuce

Reserve 1 teaspoon bacon for garnish. Combine the remaining bacon, sour cream, mayonnaise, tomatoes, parsley and lettuce in a bowl and mix well. Spoon into a serving dish. Garnish with the reserved bacon. Serve with chips. **Yield: 12 servings.**

Cha Cha Cha Black Bean Dip

2 (15-ounce) cans black beans, rinsed and drained
1 (17-ounce) can Shoe Peg corn, rinsed and drained
2 to 3 large tomatoes, peeled, seeded and chopped
1 purple onion, chopped
1/4 cup chopped fresh cilantro
1/4 cup fresh lime juice
2 tablespoons olive oil
2 tablespoons red wine vinegar
1 teaspoon salt
1/2 teaspoon pepper

Combine the beans, corn, tomatoes, onion, cilantro, lime juice, olive oil, vinegar, salt and pepper in a bowl and mix well. Chill, covered, for 24 hours. Spoon into a serving dish. Garnish with chopped avocado. Serve with tortilla chips. **Yield: 6 to 7 cups.**

BAKED BEEF DIP

2 tablespoons butter
½ cup coarsely chopped pecans
½ teaspoon salt (optional)
8 ounces cream cheese, softened
2 tablespoons milk

1 (2-ounce) jar dried chipped beef
1½ tablespoons onion flakes
1 teaspoon prepared horseradish
¼ teaspoon pepper
½ cup sour cream

Melt the butter in a skillet. Stir in the pecans and salt. Cook until the
pecans are browned, stirring constantly; do not burn. Combine the
cream cheese, milk, chipped beef, onion flakes, horseradish, pepper and
sour cream in a bowl and mix well. Spoon into a 1-quart baking dish,
spreading evenly. Sprinkle with the pecans. Bake at 350 degrees for
20 minutes. Serve with assorted crackers. **Yield: 12 servings.**

HOT REUBEN DIP

1 (18-ounce) can sauerkraut,
   rinsed and drained
8 ounces (2 cups) shredded
   Cheddar cheese

8 ounces (2 cups) shredded Swiss
   cheese
6 to 8 ounces corned beef, chopped
1 cup mayonnaise

Pat the sauerkraut with paper towels to remove any excess moisture.
Combine the sauerkraut, Cheddar cheese, Swiss cheese, corned beef and
mayonnaise in a bowl and mix well. Spoon into a 9×13-inch baking pan,
spreading evenly. Bake at 350 degrees for 30 minutes or until hot and
bubbly. Serve with cocktail rye bread or crackers. **Yield: 32 servings.**

Note: Men love this dip.

TEXAS COOL DIP

1¼ cups mayonnaise
1¼ cups sour cream
1 onion, finely chopped
2 tablespoons chopped fresh
   parsley

2 teaspoons chopped fresh dill weed
1 teaspoon seasoned salt
2 packages sliced corned beef,
   chopped
2 packages bagels, cut into wedges

Combine the mayonnaise, sour cream, onion, parsley, dill weed, seasoned salt and corned beef in a bowl and mix well. Chill, covered, for 1 hour or longer. Serve with the bagels. **Yield: 18 servings.**

Note: Children love the bagels plain, and adults devour the dip with the bagels.

ROASTED CORN GUACAMOLE

2 cups frozen corn
3 tablespoons olive oil
Juice of 1 large lime

1 cup puréed avocado
1 bunch fresh cilantro, chopped

Combine the corn and olive oil in a bowl and mix well. Spoon into a baking dish. Broil for 10 to 15 minutes or until the corn is roasted, stirring occasionally. Let stand to cool. Combine the lime juice, avocado and cilantro in a bowl and mix well. Stir into the corn mixture and mix well. Chill, covered, for 4 hours. Serve with tortilla chips. **Yield: 24 servings.**

Note: You may substitute 1 teaspoon cumin for the cilantro.

THE ULTIMATE CRAB DIP

16 ounces cream cheese, softened
1/4 cup low-fat plain yogurt
1 tablespoon prepared horseradish
1/4 teaspoon Worcestershire sauce
1/4 teaspoon ground red pepper

1/4 teaspoon hot red pepper sauce
1 tablespoon finely chopped green
　onions
1/2 cup chopped water chestnuts
1 pound lump crab meat, flaked

Beat the cream cheese at high speed in a mixing bowl until smooth. Add the yogurt, horseradish, Worcestershire sauce, red pepper and pepper sauce and beat until well mixed. Stir in the green onions, water chestnuts and crab meat. Chill until serving time. Serve with corn chips or toasted baguette slices. **Yield: 15 servings.**

SAUSALITO CRAB DIP

1 (4-ounce) package leek soup mix
1 1/2 cups sour cream or light sour
　cream
1 tablespoon lemon juice
1/8 teaspoon hot red pepper sauce
6 ounces crab meat, flaked, or
　1 cup chopped shrimp

1 (14-ounce) can artichoke hearts,
　drained and chopped
1 cup (4 ounces) shredded Swiss
　cheese
1 tablespoon chopped fresh dill
　weed, or 1 teaspoon dried
　dill weed

Combine the soup mix, sour cream, lemon juice and pepper sauce in a bowl and mix well. Stir in the crab meat, artichoke hearts, cheese and dill weed. Chill, covered, for 8 to 10 hours. Serve with crackers. **Yield: 3 3/4 cups.**

Note: This dip is also very good without the crab meat.

Spicy Spinach Dip

2 or 3 jalapeño chiles
1 medium onion, finely chopped
2 tablespoons vegetable oil
1 (4-ounce) can chopped green chiles
2 tomatoes, seeded and chopped
1 (10-ounce) package frozen chopped spinach, thawed
1½ tablespoons red wine vinegar
8 ounces cream cheese, softened
2½ cups (10 ounces) shredded Monterey Jack cheese
1 cup half-and-half
Salt and pepper to taste
Paprika

Chop the jalapeño chiles, including the seeds for a spicier dip and discarding the seeds for a milder dip. Sauté the jalapeño chiles and onion in the oil in a skillet for 4 minutes or until tender. Add the undrained green chiles and tomatoes. Cook for 2 minutes, stirring constantly. Remove from the heat. Combine the jalapeño chile mixture, spinach, vinegar, cream cheese, Monterey Jack cheese, half-and-half, salt and pepper in a bowl and mix well. Spoon into a greased 10-inch baking dish. Sprinkle with paprika. Bake at 400 degrees for 20 to 25 minutes or until hot and bubbly. Serve with tortilla chips. **Yield: 20 servings.**

Note: An easy way to seed tomatoes is to cut them into halves and squeeze out the seeds.

Saucy Strawberry Salsa

6 tablespoons olive oil
3 tablespoons white balsamic
   vinegar
1/2 tablespoon salt
2 pints cherry tomatoes, chopped

1 pint strawberries, coarsely
   chopped
8 green onions, chopped
1/2 cup fresh cilantro, chopped

Combine the olive oil, vinegar and salt in a large bowl and whisk until well blended. Add the tomatoes, strawberries, green onions and cilantro and mix well. Chill, covered, for 1 hour or longer. Serve with tortilla chips. **Yield: 5 to 6 cups.**

Sun-Dried Tomato Dip

1/4 cup oil-pack sun-dried
   tomatoes, drained and chopped
8 ounces cream cheese, softened
1/2 cup sour cream
1/2 cup mayonnaise

3 or 4 dashes of hot red pepper
   sauce
1 teaspoon kosher salt
3/4 teaspoon pepper
2 scallions, thinly sliced

Combine the sun-dried tomatoes, cream cheese, sour cream, mayonnaise, pepper sauce, kosher salt and pepper in a food processor. Process until puréed. Add the scallions and pulse 2 times. Spoon into a serving dish. Serve with crackers; Ritz Air Crisps are preferred. **Yield: 12 servings.**

Note: The ingredients for this dip are so easy to have stocked in your pantry, and the dip is so yummy.

NOT THE SAME OLD HOMEMADE BLOODY MARY

3 tablespoons vodka
2 dashes of Worcestershire sauce
4 dashes of hot red pepper sauce
1 teaspoon grated fresh horseradish
Freshly ground pepper to taste
Dash of celery salt
½ cup tomato juice
2 tablespoons orange juice
1 teaspoon vinegar (optional)

Combine the vodka, Worcestershire sauce, pepper sauce, horseradish, pepper, celery salt, tomato juice, orange juice and vinegar in a pitcher and mix well. Serve in a glass over ice. Garnish with a lime wedge, lemon wedge, celery rib or cucumber wedge. **Yield: 1 serving.**

Note: Do not dismiss the orange juice addition. It comes from the popular Mexican sangrita style.

Mango Texas Margaritas

1 very ripe large mango, peeled
1 (6-ounce) can frozen limeade
    concentrate, partially thawed
1 limeade can Jose Cuervo Gold
    Tequila

⅓ limeade can Triple Sec
1 lime, cut into 4 slices

Cut the mango into medium pieces. Combine the mango, limeade concentrate, tequila and liqueur in a blender. Process just until the mango is puréed. Add enough ice to fill the blender. Process until well blended. Serve in margarita glasses. Squeeze the juice from 1 lime slice into each glass. **Yield: 4 servings.**

Mint Tea

8 cups water
14 sprigs (or more) of fresh mint
3 family-size tea bags

1 cup sugar
¾ cup lemon juice
4 cups orange juice

Bring the water to a boil in a large saucepan. Remove from the heat. Add the mint and tea bags. Steep for 15 minutes. Remove and discard the mint and tea bags. Add the sugar and stir until dissolved. Pour into a clean 1-gallon milk jug. Add the lemon juice, orange juice and enough additional water to fill the jug. Chill, covered, until serving time. Shake well before serving. **Yield: 1 gallon.**

Note: Mint Tea is wonderful to take to receptions of any kind.

FROM SHUTTLE BOAT
TO AMPHI CAR

In the early days of the lake, there were very few telephones. To reach a lake resident, someone would call Hall's Boathouse or Rabun Boathouse and they would send someone to the house with the message. Also many homes on the back side of the lake could not be reached by road. A shuttle boat service from Hall's Boathouse or Rabun Boathouse carried homeowners, luggage, visitors, and supplies to these homes. One house even had a paved ramp into the lake where their "Amphi car" could drive from the lake up to the house. It was a sight to see that little car loaded with suitcases driving down the lake with its propellers spinning in the back.

Some favorite early pastimes at Lake Rabun were fishing, playing cards, horseshoes, badminton, working puzzles, playing charades, reading, and family picnics to Minnihaha Waterfall. A number of families in the early days would bring servants to the lake. "Hop-In" was a special place for the servants which provided entertainment on Thursday and Sunday nights.

DELICIOUS PUMPKIN, BLACK BEAN AND TURKEY SOUP

¼ cup vegetable oil
1 large onion, minced
6 garlic cloves, minced
1 yellow bell pepper, chopped
1 jalapeño chile, seeded and
　chopped
1 tablespoon each cumin, oregano
　and chili powder
6 cups beef broth
4 cups drained rinsed canned
　black beans

1 (28-ounce) can crushed tomatoes
1 (15-ounce) can puréed pumpkin
　or squash
5 cups coarsely chopped cooked
　turkey
1 cup cream sherry
Salt and freshly ground pepper
　to taste
1 medium pumpkin
　(about 12 pounds)
2 tablespoons vegetable oil

Heat ¼ cup oil in a large stockpot over medium-high heat. Add the onion, garlic, bell pepper and jalapeño chile. Sauté for 10 minutes or until tender. Stir in the cumin, oregano and chili powder. Cook for 1 minute, stirring constantly. Add the broth, beans, tomatoes, puréed pumpkin, turkey and sherry and mix well. Bring to a boil, stirring occasionally. Season with salt and pepper. Simmer for 45 minutes, stirring occasionally.

Remove the top from the pumpkin, reserving the top. Scrape out the seeds and strings and discard. Brush the inside of the pumpkin with 2 tablespoons oil. Place in a roasting pan. Fill the pan with enough water to reach 2 inches up the side of the pumpkin. Ladle the soup into the pumpkin. Replace the top of the pumpkin. Bake at 350 degrees for 1 hour or until the pumpkin is tender. Remove the pumpkin carefully to a serving plate. Ladle the soup into soup bowls. Garnish with shredded Cheddar cheese and sour cream. You may include some of the jalapeño chile seeds if a hotter soup is desired. **Yield: 12 servings.**

Note: This is an unusual combination that works.

CHICKEN AND SAUSAGE GUMBO

1 cup vegetable oil
1 (3- to 4-pound) chicken, cut into
    8 pieces
3/4 cup flour
2 cups chopped onions
1 cup chopped green bell pepper
2 ribs celery, chopped
2 tablespoons minced garlic
1 1/2 pounds andouille, sliced
1/2 cup thinly sliced green onions

2 tablespoons chopped fresh
    parsley
2 1/2 quarts chicken stock
2 teaspoons pepper
2 tablespoons hot red pepper sauce
1 1/2 teaspoons thyme
1 1/2 teaspoons basil
1 1/2 teaspoons oregano
3 bay leaves
3 cups sliced frozen okra

Heat the oil in an 8-quart stockpot over high heat. Brown the chicken in
the hot oil, turning occasionally. Remove to a plate. Add the flour to the
oil. Cook until medium brown, stirring constantly. Remove from the
heat. Stir in the onions, bell pepper, celery, garlic and sausage. Return
to the heat. Cook over medium-high heat. Add the green onions and
parsley and mix well. Add the stock gradually, whisking constantly.
Add the pepper, pepper sauce, thyme, basil, oregano, bay leaves, okra
and chicken. Simmer over medium-low heat for 45 minutes, stirring
occasionally. Remove and discard the bay leaves. Ladle into soup bowls.
Serve with hot cooked fluffy white rice and crusty French bread.
Yield: 24 servings.

*Note: If andouille is unavailable, use smoked kielbasa or any smoked meat you
can find. Filé powder is the powdered root of the sassafras tree and if used to
thicken the gumbo, it should be added just before serving. Since you are dying
to know the derivation of the word gumbo, it comes from the African word
gombo, meaning okra.*

From McKinnon's Louisiane Restaurant, Atlanta, Georgia,
Bill Glendinning, chef

Old-Fashioned Brunswick Stew

6 large chicken breasts
6 to 8 chicken thighs
3 cans chicken broth
1/2 cup chopped celery
1/2 cup chopped Vidalia onion
1/4 cup finely chopped carrots
1 tablespoon minced garlic
1 bay leaf
1 (3- to 4-pound) beef roast
1 (3- to 4-pound) pork roast
2 cans chicken broth
1 can beef broth
1/2 cup chopped celery
1/2 chopped Vidalia onion
1/4 cup finely chopped
   carrots
1 tablespoon minced garlic
1 bay leaf
1 (16-ounce) package frozen
   Shoe Peg corn

1 (16-ounce) package frozen white
   creamed corn
1/2 cup white vinegar
1/4 cup Worcestershire sauce
1 teaspoon poultry seasoning
1/4 teaspoon allspice
1 teaspoon white pepper
1 teaspoon black pepper
1/4 teaspoon red pepper
1 teaspoon hot red pepper sauce
3 (15-ounce) cans diced tomatoes
2 (15-ounce) cans tomato sauce
2 large sweet onions, chopped
1/2 cup (1 stick) butter
1/4 cup packed brown sugar
Juice of 2 lemons
Juice of 1 lime
1/4 cup (or more) hickory smoke
   barbecue sauce
Salt to taste

Combine the chicken, 3 cans chicken broth, 1/2 cup celery, 1/2 cup Vidalia onion, 1/4 cup carrots, 1 tablespoon garlic, 1 bay leaf and enough water to cover in a stockpot. Bring to a boil. Cook until the chicken is cooked through. Drain, reserving the broth and vegetables and discarding the bay leaf. Let the chicken stand to cool. Chop the chicken, discarding the skin and bones. Let the reserved broth and vegetables stand to cool. Skim off the fat. Cut the beef and pork into 1-inch pieces. Combine the beef, pork, 2 cans chicken broth, beef broth, 1/2 cup celery, 1/2 cup Vidalia onion, 1/4 cup carrots, 1 tablespoon garlic, 1 bay leaf and enough water to cover in a separate stockpot. Bring to a boil.

Cook until the beef and pork are cooked through. Drain, reserving the broth and vegetables and discarding the bay leaf. Let the beef and pork stand to cool. Let the reserved broth and vegetables stand to cool. Skim off the fat. Process the chicken, beef and pork with a small amount of the reserved broth in batches in a food processor until uniformly chopped, reserving the remaining broth. Spoon into a stockpot. Add the reserved vegetables, Shoe Peg corn, creamed corn, vinegar, Worcestershire sauce, poultry seasoning, allspice, white pepper, black pepper, red pepper, pepper sauce, tomatoes, tomato sauce, sweet onions, butter, brown sugar, lemon juice, lime juice, barbecue sauce and salt and mix well. Cook for several hours, adding small amounts of the reserved broth and water as needed and stirring occasionally; do not burn. Ladle into soup bowls. **Yield: 36 servings.**

Note: This recipe has been modernized, but it originated in Virginia during the Revolutionary War. It is well worth the effort and freezes well.

Grandma's Chicken Noodle Soup

1 (3- to 4-pound) chicken,
    cut into halves
2 ribs celery, cut into halves
1 large onion, cut into quarters
1 carrot, peeled and cut into
    halves
2 garlic cloves, crushed
1 teaspoon salt
$1/2$ teaspoon pepper
$1/4$ teaspoon tarragon

4 cups water
3 cups chicken broth
1 large onion, chopped
2 ribs celery, sliced
2 carrots, sliced
4 ounces medium egg noodles
$1/2$ teaspoon salt
$1/2$ teaspoon pepper
$1/4$ teaspoon tarragon

Combine the chicken, celery halves, onion quarters, carrot halves, garlic, 1 teaspoon salt, $1/2$ teaspoon pepper, $1/4$ teaspoon tarragon, 4 cups water and broth in a Dutch oven. Bring to a boil over high heat. Reduce the heat to low. Cook for 45 minutes or until the chicken is tender. Remove the chicken, reserving the broth mixture. Let the chicken stand to cool. Chop the chicken, discarding the skin and bones. Strain the broth mixture into a large bowl; discard the cooked vegetables. Skim the fat from the broth. Return the broth to the Dutch oven. Add the chopped onion, sliced celery and sliced carrots. Bring to a boil over high heat. Simmer for 15 minutes. Cook the noodles using the package directions, omitting the salt; drain. Stir the noodles, chicken, $1/2$ teaspoon salt, $1/2$ teaspoon pepper and $1/4$ teaspoon tarragon into the soup. Cook until heated through, stirring occasionally. Ladle into soup bowls.
Yield: 10 servings.

FIRESIDE WHITE CHILI

4 large chicken breasts (2½ to 3 pounds)
6 cups chicken broth
2 cups chopped onions
2 tablespoons olive oil
1 (4-ounce) can chopped green chiles
1 tablespoon cumin
1 tablespoon oregano
½ teaspoon cinnamon
3 cans Great Northern beans, rinsed and drained
3 cups (12 ounces) shredded four-cheese Mexican blend

Combine the chicken and broth in a stockpot or Dutch oven. Bring to a boil. Cook until the chicken is cooked through. Drain, reserving the broth. Let the chicken stand to cool. Shred the chicken. Sauté the onions in the olive oil until tender. Add the green chiles, cumin, oregano, cinnamon and chicken and mix well. Stir in the beans gently. Add enough of the reserved broth to reach the desired consistency. Simmer for 30 minutes. Remove from the heat. Add the cheese. Cook until the cheese is melted, stirring constantly. Ladle into soup bowls. Serve with sour cream, guacamole, salsa, lime wedges and tortilla chips. **Yield: 10 servings.**

CHAMPIONSHIP CHILI

1/2 cup vegetable oil
3 medium onions, chopped
2 medium green bell peppers,
    chopped
4 large ribs celery, chopped
2 garlic cloves, minced
1/2 (or more) jalapeño chile,
    chopped
3 pounds coarsely ground beef
    chuck
2 pounds coarsely ground pork
1 (4-ounce) can chopped green
    chiles

2 (15-ounce) cans stewed tomatoes
2 (15-ounce) cans tomato sauce
2 (6-ounce) cans tomato paste
6 (16-ounce) cans red chili beans
6 ounces chili powder
2 tablespoons cumin
1 1/2 cups (about) water
12 ounces beer
2 to 3 bay leaves
2 tablespoons salt, or to taste
2 tablespoons pepper, or to taste
2 tablespoons garlic powder

Heat the oil in a heavy 12-quart stockpot. Sauté the onions, bell peppers, celery, garlic and jalapeño chile in the hot oil until tender. Add the ground chuck and ground pork. Cook until the ground chuck and ground pork are brown, stirring until crumbly; drain. Add the green chiles, stewed tomatoes, tomato sauce, tomato paste, beans, chili powder, cumin, water, beer, bay leaves, salt, pepper and garlic powder and mix well. Add enough additional water to cover. Cook over low heat for 3 hours, stirring frequently. Remove and discard the bay leaves. Serve the chili with corn bread. **Yield: 12 to 16 servings.**

Note: This is a combination of the best of the '87, '88 and '89 Chili Cook-Off Winners. You may chop the vegetables in a food processor. Chop a double amount of vegetables and keep half in the freezer for the next time you make a batch of chili.

Rainy Day Corn Chowder

¹/2 cup (1 stick) butter
6 cups chopped yellow onions (4 large onions)
¹/2 cup flour
2 teaspoons kosher salt
1 teaspoon pepper
12 cups chicken stock
6 cups coarsely chopped unpeeled potatoes (about 2 pounds)
10 cups frozen corn
2 cups half-and-half

Melt the butter in a stockpot. Sauté the onions in the butter for 10 minutes. Stir in the flour, kosher salt and pepper. Cook for 2 minutes, stirring constantly. Add the stock and potatoes and mix well. Bring to a boil. Simmer for 15 minutes, stirring occasionally. Add the corn and half-and-half. Cook for 5 minutes. Ladle into soup bowls. Garnish with crumbled bacon, shredded Cheddar cheese and/or Parmesan croutons. **Yield: 6 to 8 servings.**

Note: You may substitute the kernels from 10 ears of fresh corn for the frozen corn. Blanch the fresh corn before proceeding with the recipe. This soup is great on a rainy day or after Thanksgiving.

PICNIC CUCUMBER DILL SOUP

2 cucumbers, peeled, seeded and
    coarsely chopped
1 green onion, coarsely chopped,
    or to taste
1 tablespoon lemon juice
2 cups sour cream

1 cup half-and-half
1 tablespoon minced fresh dill
    weed
1 teaspoon salt
1/4 teaspoon pepper
1/8 teaspoon hot red pepper sauce

Combine the cucumbers, green onion and lemon juice in a blender or
food processor. Process until smooth, scraping the sides occasionally.
Pour into a large bowl. Stir in the sour cream, half-and-half, dill weed,
salt, pepper and pepper sauce. Chill, covered, for 2 hours. Ladle into
soup bowls. Garnish with sprigs of fresh dill weed. **Yield: 4 servings.**

Note: This soup is wonderful with a crusty bread. For a lighter version, you
may substitute light sour cream and fat-free half-and-half for the sour cream
and half-and-half.

SAVORY TOMATO SOUP

1 1/2 cups minced onions
3 garlic cloves, crushed
Salt to taste
1 tablespoon butter
1 tablespoon olive oil
1 teaspoon chopped fresh dill weed

Pepper to taste
6 cups undrained canned diced
    tomatoes
1 tablespoon sour cream
2 medium fresh tomatoes, chopped

Sauté the onions, garlic and salt in the butter and olive oil in a saucepan
until tender. Add the dill weed, pepper and canned tomatoes and mix
well. Simmer over low heat for 45 minutes. Remove from the heat. Stir in
the sour cream and fresh tomatoes. Garnish with chopped scallions and
yogurt. **Yield: 4 servings.**

TED'S MONTANA GRILL TOMATO BISQUE

1 cup chopped carrots
1 cup chopped celery
1 cup chopped onion
½ cup (1 stick) butter
1½ teaspoons minced garlic
5 tablespoons flour
3 (15-ounce) cans diced tomatoes
Canned tomato juice
3 cups chicken broth
2 chicken bouillon cubes
2 cups heavy cream
1 tablespoon sugar
1 teaspoon Tabasco sauce

Process the carrots, celery and onion in a food processor until minced. Melt the butter in a heavy stockpot. Add the carrot mixture and garlic. Sauté for 10 to 15 minutes or until tender. Add the flour. Reduce the heat to low. Cook for 5 minutes, stirring constantly. Drain the tomatoes, reserving the juice. Place the reserved juice in a large measuring bowl. Add enough canned tomato juice to measure 6 cups. Combine the juice, broth and bouillon in a bowl and mix well. Add gradually to the vegetable mixture, stirring constantly. Bring to a boil. Simmer for 10 minutes, scraping the bottom frequently. Stir in the tomatoes. Simmer for 5 minutes. Process in a food mill or blender until puréed. Return to the stockpot. Add the cream, sugar and Tabasco sauce and mix well. Bring to a simmer. Ladle into soup bowls. Serve with sour cream and chives. **Yield: 10 servings.**

From Ted's Montana Grill, Atlanta, Georgia

43

Lakemont Provisions' Shrimp and Corn Salad

36 small to medium shrimp
Shrimp boil to taste
Salt to taste
¾ cup olive oil
¾ cup peanut oil
¾ cup red wine vinegar
2 tablespoons whole grain mustard
2 tablespoons finely chopped garlic
2 tablespoons finely chopped chives
2 tablespoons finely chopped shallots
8 ears of corn

Peel and devein the shrimp, discarding the tails. Combine the shrimp, shrimp boil, salt and enough water to cover in a saucepan. Bring to a boil; drain. Let stand to cool. Combine the olive oil, peanut oil, vinegar, whole grain mustard, garlic, chives and shallots in a bowl and whisk to mix well. Pour over the shrimp in a bowl and mix well. Chill, covered, for 2 to 4 hours. Combine the corn and enough water to cover in a saucepan. Bring to a boil. Boil until tender. Let stand to cool. Cut the corn from the cob into a bowl. Chill, covered, until serving time. Combine the shrimp mixture and corn in a salad bowl and toss to mix. Garnish with fresh parsley. **Yield: 6 servings.**

From Lakemont Provisions, Lakemont, Georgia

SHRIMP AND GREEN BEAN SALAD

2 pounds medium shrimp, peeled and deveined
12 ounces thin tender green beans
1/4 cup chopped fresh chives
Grated zest of 1 lemon
1/2 teaspoon pepper
1/3 cup raspberry vinegar
1 teaspoon Dijon mustard
Salt and pepper to taste
1/2 cup olive oil
1 cup fresh raspberries
1 head Boston lettuce or other greens
1 tablespoon chopped fresh chives

Combine the shrimp with enough water to cover in a saucepan. Bring to a boil. Boil for 1 minute; drain. Combine the green beans and enough water to cover in a saucepan. Bring to a boil. Boil for 1 minute; drain. Dip in ice water. Drain and pat dry. Combine the shrimp and green beans in a bowl and toss to mix. Add 1/4 cup chives, lemon zest and 1/2 teaspoon pepper and mix well. Combine the vinegar and Dijon mustard in a small bowl and whisk to mix well. Add salt and pepper to taste. Add the olive oil gradually, whisking constantly until thickened. Pour over the shrimp mixture. Add half the raspberries and toss gently to mix. Arrange the lettuce leaves on a serving platter. Spoon the shrimp mixture onto the lettuce. Top with the remaining raspberries and 1 tablespoon chives. **Yield: 6 to 8 servings.**

Asian Grilled Chicken Salad

Canola oil
Thin tortilla strips
Mixed salad greens
Shredded or thinly sliced grilled
    chicken
Shredded carrots

Lime Salad Dressing
1/4 cup peanut butter
1/4 cup soy sauce
1/4 cup hot water
2 teaspoons sesame oil
1 tablespoon ginger

Heat a small amount of canola oil in a skillet. Fry the tortilla strips in the hot oil until brown; drain on paper towels. Combine the salad greens, chicken, carrots, tortillas and Lime Salad Dressing in a salad bowl and toss to mix. Combine the peanut butter, soy sauce, hot water, sesame oil and ginger in a bowl and mix well. Drizzle over the salad. Serve immediately. **Yield: 6 to 8 servings.**

Lime Salad Dressing

1/2 cup lime juice
4 teaspoons honey mustard
7 1/2 tablespoons honey
1/4 cup vegetable oil

2 garlic cloves, finely minced
1 teaspoon pepper
1/2 teaspoon salt

Combine the lime juice, honey mustard, honey, oil, garlic, pepper and salt in a bowl and mix well.

Note: This is the same recipe that is served in a very popular restaurant chain.

Tarragon Chicken Salad

4 boneless skinless chicken breasts,
    cooked and chopped
1/4 cup chopped onion
1/4 cup chopped celery
1 cup red grape halves
1/2 cup sliced almonds, lightly toasted
3 tablespoons mayonnaise
1 tablespoon chopped fresh tarragon
1 tablespoon lemon juice
Salt and pepper to taste
Lettuce leaves

Combine the chicken, onion, celery, grapes, almonds, mayonnaise, tarragon, lemon juice, salt and pepper in a bowl and toss lightly to mix. Chill, covered, for 2 to 3 hours. Serve on a bed of lettuce.
Yield: 4 to 6 servings.

Note: You may adjust the onion and tarragon to your taste.

LAYERED COBB SALAD

5 cups water
3 boneless skinless chicken breasts
    (about 1¼ pounds)
2 avocados
2 teaspoons lemon juice
1 head romaine, cut crosswise into
    ½-inch slices (about 8 cups)
6 slices bacon, crisp-cooked and
    crumbled
3 medium tomatoes, seeded and
    cut into ½-inch pieces
2 to 3 ounces Roquefort cheese
2 bunches watercress, stems
    removed

2 eggs, hard-cooked
¼ cup finely chopped fresh
    chives
3 tablespoons red wine vinegar
1 tablespoon fresh lemon juice
2 teaspoons Dijon mustard
1 small garlic clove, minced
½ teaspoon sugar
½ teaspoon salt
¼ teaspoon pepper
½ cup extra-virgin olive oil

Bring 5 cups water to a boil in a 2-quart saucepan. Add the chicken.
Simmer for 6 minutes. Remove from the heat. Let stand, covered, for
15 minutes or until the chicken is cooked through; drain. Let stand
to cool. Cut the chicken into ½-inch pieces. Cut the avocados into
½-inch pieces. Combine the avocados and 2 teaspoons lemon juice
in a bowl and mix well. Spread the romaine in the bottom of a 6- to
8-quart glass salad bowl. Layer the chicken, bacon, tomatoes, cheese,
avocados, watercress, eggs and chives in the bowl. Combine the vinegar,
1 tablespoon lemon juice, Dijon mustard, garlic, sugar, salt and pepper
in a bowl and whisk to mix well. Add the olive oil gradually, whisking
constantly until emulsified. Pour the dressing over the salad and toss to
mix well. Serve immediately. **Yield: 4 to 6 servings.**

*Note: The dressing may be made ahead and chilled, covered, until serving
time. The salad may be assembled an hour ahead and chilled, covered, until
serving time.*

CORNUCOPIA SALAD

¹/₂ cup slivered almonds
3 tablespoons sugar
1 medium head green leaf lettuce, torn
4 green onions, chopped
1 can mandarin oranges
1 avocado, sliced
1 Granny Smith apple, sliced
¹/₄ cup dried cranberries or cherries
¹/₂ cup crumbled blue cheese
Sliced grilled chicken (optional)
Oil and Vinegar Dressing

Combine the almonds and sugar in a small skillet. Cook over medium heat until the sugar dissolves and the almonds are browned, stirring constantly. Remove to foil to cool. Combine the lettuce, green onions, mandarin oranges, avocado, apple, cranberries, cheese, toasted almonds and chicken in a salad bowl. Add Oil and Vinegar Dressing and toss to mix. **Yield: 6 servings.**

OIL AND VINEGAR DRESSING

¹/₄ cup vegetable oil
2 tablespoons white wine vinegar
1 tablespoon finely chopped fresh parsley
2 tablespoons sugar
¹/₂ teaspoon salt
¹/₂ teaspoon pepper

Combine the oil, vinegar, parsley, sugar, salt and pepper in a jar with a tight-fitting lid and shake to mix well.

Buck Creek Salad

Chopped romaine hearts
Crumbled blue cheese
Pecans

Croutons
Buck Creek Dressing

Combine the lettuce, cheese, pecans and croutons in a salad bowl. Add Buck Creek Dressing and toss to mix. **Yield: 36 servings.**

Buck Creek Dressing

4 garlic cloves
1 cup dried Mission figs
1/4 cup olive oil
1 cup dried dates
1/4 cup olive oil
1 cup raisins

1/4 cup olive oil
1 cup packed brown sugar
1 1/4 cups olive oil
1/4 cup balsamic vinegar
Salt and pepper to taste

Process the garlic in a blender until chopped. Add the figs and 1/4 cup olive oil and process for 30 seconds. Add the dates and 1/4 cup olive oil and process until blended. Add the raisins and 1/4 cup olive oil and process until blended. Add the brown sugar, 1 1/4 cups olive oil, vinegar, salt and pepper and process until blended. You may need to process the ingredients in batches. Store dressing in jars with tight-fitting lids in the refrigerator.

From Buck Creek Tavern, Clayton, Georgia

Mixed Greens with Pears and Gorgonzola

Mixed salad greens
1/2 bunch green onions, chopped
2 pears or Granny Smith apples
1/2 cup crumbled Gorgonzola cheese
1/2 cup walnuts
Red Wine Vinaigrette

Combine the salad greens, green onions, pears, cheese and walnuts in a salad bowl. Add Red Wine Vinaigrette and toss to mix. Serve immediately. **Yield: 6 to 8 servings.**

Red Wine Vinaigrette

1/3 cup red wine vinegar
1/3 cup sugar
1 teaspoon salt
1 teaspoon dry mustard
1 teaspoon minced garlic
2/3 cup vegetable oil

Combine the vinegar, sugar, salt, dry mustard, garlic and oil in a jar with a tight-fitting lid and shake to mix well.

Note: It is best to make the salad dressing in advance to allow the flavors to marry.

WEDGE SALAD WITH BACON, TOMATO AND CHIVE DRESSING

1 envelope ranch salad dressing mix
1 cup milk
1 cup mayonnaise
1/3 cup chopped fresh chives
1/4 cup chopped tomatoes
1/4 cup crumbled cooked bacon
1 1/2 teaspoons warm bacon drippings
2 heads iceberg lettuce

Combine the salad dressing mix, milk and mayonnaise in a medium bowl and prepare using the package directions. Add the chives, tomatoes, bacon and bacon drippings and mix well. Chill, covered, until serving time. Cut each head of lettuce into 6 wedges. Place on salad plates. Spoon 2 ounces of salad dressing over each wedge. Garnish with additional chives, tomatoes and bacon. **Yield: 12 servings.**

Note: This salad dressing is best when made 2 hours before using.

From Ted's Montana Grill, Atlanta, Georgia

Light Asparagus Vinaigrette

2 bunches asparagus
1/2 cup vinegar
1/2 cup water
2 tablespoons chopped fresh
parsley

2 tablespoons chopped fresh chives
2 tablespoons Dijon mustard
1/2 teaspoon tarragon
8 ounces baby spinach

Combine the asparagus and enough water to cover in a saucepan. Cook until the asparagus is tender; drain. Arrange in a shallow bowl. Combine the vinegar, water, parsley, chives, Dijon mustard and tarragon in a bowl and mix well. Pour the dressing over the asparagus. Chill, covered, for 3 to 5 hours. Arrange the spinach on a serving plate. Top with the asparagus. Pour the dressing over the asparagus. Garnish with cherry tomatoes. Serve immediately. **Yield: 6 servings.**

Black Bean and Rice Salad

2 cups cooked rice
1 (15-ounce) can black beans,
rinsed and drained

1 medium jar salsa
2 cups sour cream

Combine the rice, beans, salsa and sour cream in a bowl and mix well. Spoon into a salad bowl. Chill, covered, for 8 hours. **Yield: 6 to 8 servings.**

Note: This recipe is easily doubled.

Green Bean Salad

2 (15-ounce) cans French-style
    green beans, drained
3/4 cup sliced green olives
3/4 cup sliced black olives
3/4 cup chopped pecans
3/4 cup chopped red bell pepper
3/4 cup chopped yellow bell pepper
1/2 cup chopped green onions

1/2 rib celery, chopped
1 1/2 cups vegetable oil
1/2 cup vinegar
2 teaspoons salt
1/4 teaspoon pepper
1/4 teaspoon paprika
1/2 teaspoon dry mustard

Combine the green beans, green olives, black olives, pecans, bell
peppers, green onions and celery in a bowl and mix well. Combine the
oil, vinegar, salt, pepper, paprika and dry mustard in a bowl and mix
well. Pour over the green bean mixture and mix well. Chill, covered, for
several hours. Drain well before serving. **Yield: 8 servings.**

Oriental Coleslaw

1 cup vegetable oil
1/2 cup sugar
1/3 cup white vinegar
2 packages beef-flavor ramen
    noodles
1 cup sunflower seeds, toasted

1 cup slivered almonds, toasted
1 bunch green onions, chopped
2 carrots, grated
1 (16-ounce) package mixed sliced
    cabbage

Combine the oil, sugar, vinegar and seasoning from the ramen noodles
in a bowl and mix well. Chill, covered, for several hours. Crumble the
ramen noodles into a bowl. Add the sunflower seeds, almonds and
green onions and mix well. Combine the carrots, cabbage, ramen noodle
mixture and dressing in a salad bowl and toss to coat. Serve immediately.
Yield: 12 servings.

LAYERED SOUTHWESTERN SALAD

1/3 cup fresh cilantro
1/2 cup lime juice
1/2 cup olive oil
1/2 cup sour cream
1 teaspoon sugar
1/2 teaspoon salt
1/2 teaspoon pepper
1 pound romaine, shredded
5 plum tomatoes, chopped
1 (15-ounce) can black beans, rinsed and drained
1 small purple onion, chopped
2 cups (8 ounces) shredded three-cheese Mexican blend
1 (15-ounce) can Mexicorn, drained
1 (6-ounce) can sliced black olives, drained
2 cups crushed tortilla chips

Combine the cilantro, lime juice, olive oil, sour cream, sugar, salt and
pepper in a blender or food processor. Process the dressing until smooth,
scraping sides as needed. Layer the romaine, tomatoes, beans, onion,
cheese, Mexicorn, black olives and tortilla chips in a 3-quart glass bowl.
Pour the dressing over the salad and toss gently to mix. Garnish with
additional fresh cilantro. Serve immediately. **Yield: 8 to 10 servings.**

ARCADIAN SPRINGS POTATO SALAD

2 pounds red potatoes, scrubbed
1 teaspoon salt
3/4 cup chopped celery
1/2 cup chopped Vidalia onion
3 eggs, hard-cooked and chopped
3/4 to 1 cup mayonnaise
2 tablespoons prepared mustard
1/3 cup dill pickle relish
Salt and pepper to taste
Paprika (optional)

Combine the potatoes, salt and enough cold water to cover in a 3-quart saucepan. Bring to a simmer. Simmer for 15 to 25 minutes or until tender; drain. Let stand to cool slightly. Peel the potatoes and cut into 1/2-inch pieces. Combine the potatoes, celery, onion, eggs, mayonnaise, prepared mustard and pickle relish in a bowl and mix gently. Stir in salt and pepper. Spoon into a salad bowl. Chill, covered, until serving time. Sprinkle with paprika and serve. **Yield: 6 to 8 servings.**

Authentic German Potato Salad

6 medium potatoes, scrubbed
1 medium onion, finely chopped
¹/₂ rib celery, finely chopped
6 slices bacon
³/₄ cup sugar
¹/₂ cup vinegar
¹/₂ cup apple cider or apple juice
1 teaspoon salt
¹/₂ teaspoon pepper
¹/₄ teaspoon celery seeds

Combine the potatoes and enough water to cover in a 3-quart saucepan. Bring to a boil. Boil until the potatoes are tender; drain. Let stand until cool. Peel the potatoes and cut into ¹/₂-inch slices. You may use an egg slicer to cut the potatoes. Combine the potatoes, onion and celery in a bowl and mix gently. Cook the bacon in a skillet until crisp. Remove the bacon to a plate with a slotted spoon. Add the sugar, vinegar, apple cider, salt, pepper and celery seeds to the bacon drippings and mix gently. Pour over the potato mixture and mix gently. Crumble the bacon. Add to the potato mixture and mix gently. Let stand for 1 to 2 hours. Sprinkle with a small amount of hot water and mix gently. Serve immediately. **Yield: 12 servings.**

Note: This recipe comes from the contributor's grandmother, who was from Dresden, Germany, and came through Ellis Island in the late 1800s.

Tortellini Salad

32 ounces good-quality fresh assorted tortellini
1 head broccoli, broken into florets
1 pound carrots, sliced
3 leeks, cut into thin strips
2 large red bell peppers, julienned
2 large green bell peppers, julienned
2 large yellow bell peppers, julienned
1/2 cup chopped fresh basil
2 tablespoons fresh lemon juice
1 tablespoon Dijon mustard
1 tablespoon balsamic vinegar
1 cup vegetable oil
1/2 cup olive oil
1 teaspoon thyme
Salt and pepper to taste

Cook the tortellini using the package directions; drain. Place in a large bowl. Combine the broccoli, carrots and enough water to cover in a saucepan. Bring to a boil. Boil just until tender; drain. Add to the tortellini. Combine the leeks and enough water to cover in a saucepan. Bring to a boil. Boil for 1 minute. Rinse with cold water. Add the leeks, bell peppers and basil to the pasta mixture. Combine the lemon juice, Dijon mustard and vinegar in a food processor. Process for 30 seconds. Add the vegetable oil and olive oil gradually, processing constantly. Add the thyme, salt and pepper and process until blended. Pour over the salad. Serve at room temperature. **Yield: 10 servings.**

GREEK PASTA SALAD

8 ounces vermicelli
1 (2-ounce) can sliced black olives
2 ounces diced pimentos, drained
5 green onions, chopped
1/2 cup olive oil
1/4 cup mayonnaise
3 tablespoons lemon juice
2 teaspoons (heaping) Cavender's Greek Seasoning
Feta cheese with basil and tomatoes to taste, crumbled

Break the vermicelli into thirds. Cook using the package directions; drain. Combine the vermicelli, black olives, pimentos and green onions in a salad bowl. Combine the olive oil, mayonnaise, lemon juice and seasoning in a bowl and mix well. Pour over the salad and mix well. Sprinkle with the cheese. Serve immediately. **Yield: 6 servings.**

Note: You may add cooked shrimp or grilled chicken for a main dish salad. Cavender's Greek Seasoning is found in the spice section of most grocery stores.

HOT MACARONI SALAD

7 ounces shell macaroni
6 slices bacon
2 tablespoons white vinegar
1 tablespoon finely chopped onion
1/2 teaspoon salt
1/4 teaspoon pepper
1/2 teaspoon prepared mustard
1/3 cup mayonnaise
1/2 cup chopped green bell pepper
1/4 cup chopped celery
1/4 cup chopped fresh parsley

Cook the macaroni using the package directions; drain. Cook the bacon until tender-crisp; drain, reserving the drippings. Add the vinegar, onion, salt and pepper to the drippings and mix well. Bring to a boil. Remove from the heat. Add the macaroni, mustard, mayonnaise, bell pepper, celery and parsley and toss to mix. Spoon into a salad bowl. Serve immediately. **Yield: 4 to 6 servings.**

Note: Everyone loves this salad. It is great for lunch or Sunday night supper.

CAESAR SALAD DRESSING

1 cup mayonnaise
⅔ cup sour cream
1 (2-ounce) can anchovy fillets,
    drained
⅓ cup minced fresh parsley
3 tablespoons chopped green
    onions

2 tablespoons tarragon vinegar
2 tablespoons lemon juice
⅓ garlic clove, chopped
½ teaspoon salt

Combine the mayonnaise, sour cream, anchovies, parsley, green onions, vinegar, lemon juice, garlic and salt in a blender or food processor. Process until well mixed. Spoon into a bowl. Chill, covered, until serving time. **Yield: 8 to 10 servings.**

Note: This salad dressing is best if used the same day or the next day.

POPPY SEED DRESSING

2 teaspoons dry mustard
2 teaspoons salt
1½ cups sugar
3 tablespoons grated onion

⅔ cup white or apple cider
    vinegar
2 cups corn oil
3 tablespoons poppy seeds

Combine the dry mustard, salt, sugar, onion, vinegar, corn oil and poppy seeds in a blender. Process until well mixed. **Yield: 2½ cups.**

Note: The recipe may be halved. This is a great dressing for avocado and grapefruit salad, and it keeps well.

FROM BOAT RACING
TO AQUAPLANING

Boat racing was also an early sporting event and was often held at the end of Witham Point. The Lakemont Boating Club was formed by a group of avid boating enthusiasts. "Miss Barbara," "Bumpy," and "Miss Marge" were some early boats on the lake. Some boats could even be recognized by the distinctive sound of their motors. The John Lundeen family still owns and uses the oldest original boat delivered to Lakemont, a 1932 Triple Cockpit Chris-Craft.

Wool bathing suits were the lake fashion in the 1930s as well as a new water sport called aquaplaning. You would stand or sit on a large wooden board tied by a rope to the back of a boat. The speed of the boat allowed the aquaplane to glide across the top of the water.

MEAT AND PASTA DISHES

BEEF TENDERLOIN À LA LAKE

2 ounces pepper
1 cup soy sauce
3/4 cup red wine vinegar
1 tablespoon ketchup
1 teaspoon paprika
1/2 teaspoon garlic powder
1 (4- to 6-pound) beef tenderloin

Combine the pepper, soy sauce, vinegar, ketchup, paprika and garlic powder in a bowl and mix well. Pour into a large sealable plastic bag. Add the tenderloin. Marinate in the refrigerator for 8 to 10 hours. Remove the tenderloin to a baking dish, discarding the marinade. Let the tenderloin stand until it reaches room temperature. Bake at 475 degrees for 20 minutes. Reduce the oven temperature to 325 degrees. Bake for 5 minutes. Cut into slices and serve. **Yield: 10 to 12 servings.**

Note: You may sauté onions and mushrooms to serve over the tenderloin.

MARINATED CHUCK ROAST

1 (3- to 5-pound) chuck roast
Meat tenderizer
1/2 cup strong coffee
1/2 cup soy sauce
1 tablespoon Worcestershire sauce
1 tablespoon vinegar
1 large onion, chopped

Place the roast in a shallow dish. Sprinkle with meat tenderizer. Combine the coffee, soy sauce, Worcestershire sauce, vinegar and onion in a bowl and mix well. Pour over the roast; cover. Marinate in the refrigerator for 8 to 10 hours, turning occasionally. Remove from the marinade. Grill for 45 minutes or until cooked through. **Yield: 4 to 6 servings.**

Note: This is a favorite of family and friends. It would make great leftovers, but there is never any left to freeze.

Pepper-Seared New York Strip

1 (12-ounce) New York strip steak
1/2 teaspoon seasoned salt
1/2 teaspoon cracked pepper
1 tablespoon olive oil
1 tablespoon minced shallots
1/2 cup brandy
1/2 cup heavy cream
1/2 cup veal stock
1/4 teaspoon chopped fresh thyme
1/4 teaspoon salt
Pinch of white pepper

Sprinkle the steak with the seasoned salt. Rub the cracked pepper over 1 side of the steak. Heat the olive oil in an ovenproof skillet over high heat. Place the steak pepper side down in the skillet. Cook for 1 to 2 minutes per side or until seared. Bake at 300 degrees for 15 minutes for medium rare. Remove the steak to a plate; keep warm. Pour off most of the pan drippings. Sauté the shallots in the remaining pan drippings until tender. Add the brandy, cream and stock. Cook until reduced, stirring constantly. Add the thyme, salt and white pepper and mix well. Pour over the steak. **Yield: 1 serving.**

From Chops/Lobster Bar, Atlanta Georgia

Marinated Flank Steak

1 flank steak or London broil
1 tablespoon lemon juice
½ cup soy sauce
1 tablespoon Worcestershire sauce
1 teaspoon sugar
½ garlic clove, crushed
2 tablespoons brandy or bourbon
Dash of Tabasco sauce
Dash of ginger

Place the steak in a shallow dish. Combine the lemon juice, soy sauce, Worcestershire sauce, sugar, garlic, brandy, Tabasco sauce and ginger in a bowl and mix well. Pour over the steak; cover. Marinate in the refrigerator for 4 to 6 hours. Remove from the marinade. Grill over medium heat for 5 to 7 minutes per side for medium rare. Cut diagonally into thin slices and serve. **Yield: 4 servings.**

Note: This was demonstrated by Burt Reynolds on the Dinah Shore television show in the late 1970s. It is great for dinner parties.

WONDERFUL MEAT LOAF

2 hot sausage links
1¼ pounds ground round
⅔ pound ground veal
1 bottle chili sauce
2 eggs, beaten
½ shallot, chopped
½ medium onion, chopped
½ green bell pepper, chopped
1 to 2 garlic cloves, chopped
1 to 2 teaspoons Worcestershire sauce
1 tablespoon Creole seasoning
1 teaspoon fennel seeds, partially ground
½ teaspoon hot red pepper flakes, partially ground

Remove the casings from the sausage. Crumble the sausage into a large bowl. Add the ground round, ground veal, half the chili sauce, eggs, shallot, onion, bell pepper, garlic, Worcestershire sauce, Creole seasoning, fennel seeds and red pepper flakes and mix well. Shape into 2 small loaves or 1 large loaf and place in loaf pans. Pour the remaining chili sauce over the top. Sprinkle with additional Creole seasoning. Bake at 350 degrees for 30 to 45 minutes. **Yield: 8 servings.**

Note: A very tasty variation on meat loaf, this recipe is highly recommended.

TIPSY PORK TENDERLOIN WITH MUSTARD SAUCE

1 pork tenderloin
³/4 cup bourbon
³/4 cup light soy sauce
1 bunch green onions, sliced
³/4 cup mayonnaise
³/4 cup sour cream
1 tablespoon (heaping) dry mustard
1 bunch green onions, sliced

Pierce the surface of the pork with a fork. Place in a nonreactive baking dish. Combine the bourbon, soy sauce and 1 bunch green onions in a bowl and mix well. Pour over the pork. Marinate, covered, in the refrigerator for 8 to 10 hours, turning occasionally. Let stand at room temperature for 30 to 45 minutes. Bake, uncovered, at 350 degrees for 30 to 45 minutes or until cooked through. Combine the mayonnaise, sour cream, dry mustard and 1 bunch green onions in a bowl and mix well. Serve with the pork. **Yield: 6 servings.**

Pork Tenderloin with Apricot Sauce

2 tablespoons dry mustard
2 teaspoons chopped fresh thyme, or 1¼ teaspoons dried thyme
½ cup dry sherry
½ cup soy sauce
2 garlic cloves, minced
1 (4-pound) pork tenderloin or pork loin roast
1 (10-ounce) jar apricot preserves
1 tablespoon soy sauce
2 tablespoons dry sherry

Combine the dry mustard, thyme, ½ cup sherry, ½ cup soy sauce and garlic in a sealable plastic bag and shake to mix well. Add the pork. Marinate in the refrigerator for 3 to 10 hours. Remove the pork from the marinade. Place on a rack in a shallow roasting pan. Bake at 325 degrees until a meat thermometer registers 170 degrees. Combine the apricot preserves, 1 tablespoon soy sauce and 2 tablespoons sherry in a saucepan and mix well. Bring to a simmer. Simmer for 30 minutes, stirring frequently. Serve over the pork. **Yield: 8 servings.**

Spicy Slow-Cooker Pork

1 (3-pound) Boston pork butt roast
1 teaspoon cumin
$1/2$ teaspoon seasoned salt
Salt and pepper to taste
2 tablespoons vegetable oil
1 (15-ounce) can Mexican-style tomatoes
1 envelope taco seasoning mix
1 (7-ounce) can chipotle chiles in adobo sauce, or to taste
2 to 3 tablespoons cornstarch
1 (8-count) can jumbo corn muffin biscuits

Sprinkle the roast with cumin, seasoned salt, salt and pepper. Brown on all sides in the oil in a saucepan. Remove to a slow cooker. Combine the undrained tomatoes, taco seasoning mix, adobo sauce and half the chipotle chiles in a bowl and mix well. Pour over the roast. Cook, covered, on Low for 8 to 10 hours or on High for 4 to 5 hours. Remove the roast to a plate. Shred the roast; keep warm. Cook the sauce in the slow cooker on High until hot. Combine the cornstarch and a small amount of the sauce in a bowl and mix well. Stir the mixture into the sauce. Cook the biscuits using the package directions. Cut the biscuits into halves and place on individual serving plates. Serve the pork and sauce over the biscuits. **Yield: 8 servings.**

Note: This dish goes well with corn on the cob and a green vegetable. Adjust the heat of the sauce by using more or less chipotle chiles.

HOLIDAY HAM TOWERS

3 cups chopped ham
1 onion, chopped (about ½ cup)
2 tablespoons butter
¼ cup sliced black olives
1 (10-ounce) can reduced-fat cream of celery soup
1 cup reduced-fat sour cream
⅓ cup 2% milk
½ teaspoon paprika
6 puff pastry shells
⅓ cup slivered almonds, toasted

Cook the ham and onion in the butter in a skillet until tender. Stir in the black olives. Combine the soup, sour cream, milk and paprika in a bowl and mix well. Add to the ham mixture. Cook until heated through, stirring frequently. Bake the pastry shells using the package directions. Spoon equal portions of the ham mixture into each shell. Sprinkle with the almonds. **Yield: 6 servings.**

Note: Make this a new addition to your Christmas menu.

Sausage Yum-Yum

2 (28-ounce) cans diced tomatoes
3 pounds kielbasa or smoked breakfast sausage,
    cut into ¼-inch slices
3 medium green bell peppers, sliced
3 to 4 canned jalapeño chiles, seeded and chopped
Hot red pepper sauce to taste
1 tablespoon steak sauce
1 tablespoon Worcestershire sauce
½ cup beer
1 (6-ounce) can tomato paste

Drain the tomatoes, reserving the juice. Combine the tomatoes, sausage and bell peppers in a large skillet or Dutch oven and mix well. Combine the jalapeño chiles, pepper sauce, steak sauce, Worcestershire sauce, beer and tomato paste in a bowl and mix well. Pour over the sausage mixture and mix well. Bring to a simmer. Simmer for 1 hour, stirring occasionally and adding small amounts of the reserved tomato juice if needed for the desired consistency. Serve over hot cooked rice. **Yield: 8 to 10 servings.**

Note: For an excellent appetizer, serve the sausage with wooden picks.

Bison Meat Loaf

1 medium onion
1/2 green bell pepper
1/2 yellow bell pepper
1/2 red bell pepper
2 tablespoons butter
1 cup herb-seasoned stuffing mix
2 eggs, lightly beaten
2 tablespoons water
6 tablespoons grated Parmesan cheese
Salt and pepper to taste
1/8 teaspoon hot red pepper sauce
2 pounds ground bison

Chop the onion and bell peppers. Sauté in the butter in a skillet just until tender. Combine the onion mixture, stuffing mix, eggs, water, cheese, salt, pepper and pepper sauce in a large bowl and mix well. Add the ground bison and mix well. Shape into a loaf. Place in an 8×13-inch baking dish. Bake at 350 degrees for 35 to 40 minutes or until cooked through; do not overcook. **Yield: 6 to 8 servings.**

Note: Bison has less fat and cholesterol than chicken and some fish. It is hearty and delicious.

RACK OF LAMB

1 (1½-pound) rack of lamb
3 tablespoons Dijon mustard
½ cup fresh bread crumbs
¼ cup chopped fresh parsley
1 teaspoon chopped fresh rosemary
1 garlic clove, pressed

Spread the rib side of the lamb with 1 tablespoon of the Dijon mustard. Combine the remaining Dijon mustard, bread crumbs, parsley, rosemary and garlic in a bowl and mix well. Spread over the other side of the lamb. Bake at 450 degrees for 10 minutes. Reduce the oven temperature to 400 degrees. Bake for 25 minutes. **Yield: 3 servings.**

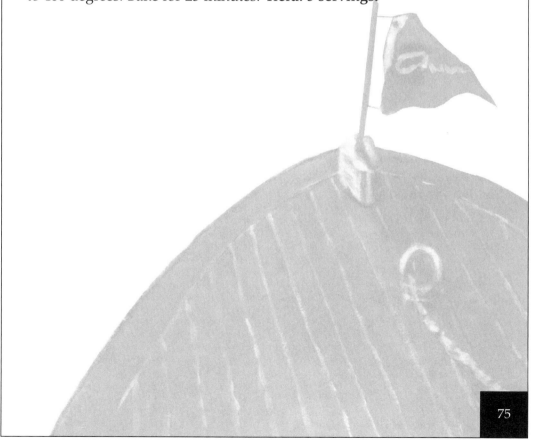

PEPPER-CRUSTED LEG OF LAMB

3 tablespoons crushed mixed white, black and
    green peppercorns
1 tablespoon fresh rosemary, chopped, or
    1¹/₂ teaspoons dried rosemary
¹/₂ cup fresh mint leaves, chopped
3 garlic cloves, crushed
¹/₂ cup raspberry vinegar
¹/₄ cup soy sauce
¹/₂ cup dry red wine
1 (5-pound) boneless untied leg of lamb
2 tablespoons Dijon mustard

Combine 1 tablespoon of the peppercorns, the rosemary, mint, garlic,
vinegar, soy sauce and wine in a large shallow dish and mix well. Add
the lamb; cover. Marinate in the refrigerator for 8 to 10 hours, turning
occasionally. Remove the lamb from the marinade, reserving the
marinade. Roll the lamb and tie with a string. Spread the Dijon mustard
over the lamb. Press the remaining peppercorns into the mustard. Place
in a shallow roasting pan. Pour the reserved marinade around the lamb.
Bake at 350 degrees for 18 minutes per pound for medium rare, basting
occasionally. Bake for 10 to 15 minutes longer for well done. Let stand
for 20 minutes before carving. Serve with the pan drippings.
Yield: 8 servings.

Veal Scaloppine with Mushrooms and Capers

1 (1-pound) veal round steak
    (¹/₂ inch), pounded, or
    1 pound veal scaloppine
¹/₄ cup flour
¹/₂ teaspoon salt
¹/₄ teaspoon pepper
¹/₄ cup olive oil
1 garlic clove, crushed or minced
2 tablespoons butter
8 ounces mushrooms, sliced

1 medium onion, thinly sliced
1³/₄ cups drained canned diced
    tomatoes, or
    2 cups chopped fresh tomatoes
¹/₂ teaspoon salt
¹/₂ teaspoon pepper
1 teaspoon chopped fresh parsley
¹/₂ teaspoon oregano
¹/₂ cup undrained capers
Hot cooked pasta or rice

Cut the veal into 1-inch pieces. Combine the flour, ¹/₂ teaspoon salt and
¹/₄ teaspoon pepper in a sealable plastic bag and shake to mix well. Add
the veal and shake to coat evenly. Heat the olive oil and garlic in a large
skillet. Brown the veal in the mixture, turning once; keep warm. Heat
the butter in a skillet. Sauté the mushrooms and onion in the butter until
the onion is translucent. Add to the veal in the large skillet. Add the
tomatoes, ¹/₂ teaspoon salt, ¹/₂ teaspoon pepper, parsley, oregano and
capers and mix well. Cook, covered, for 25 minutes, stirring occasionally.
Serve over pasta. **Yield: 4 servings.**

Osso Buco

8 (2½-inch) veal shanks
Salt and pepper to taste
½ cup flour
½ cup (1 stick) butter
3 tablespoons olive oil
1½ cups finely chopped onions
¾ cup finely chopped carrots
¾ cup finely chopped celery
1 tablespoon minced garlic

3 cups beef broth
1½ cups dry white wine
2 tablespoons Emeril's Original
    Seasoning
2 bay leaves
12 grape tomatoes
Hot cooked brown and wild rice
Gremolata

Season the veal with salt and pepper. Coat with the flour, shaking off any excess flour. Heat half the butter and half the olive oil in a nonstick skillet over medium heat. Brown the veal in the butter mixture, turning once. Remove to a 3-quart baking dish. Add the remaining butter and olive oil to the pan drippings. Sauté the onions, carrots, celery and garlic in the butter mixture until tender. Add the sautéed vegetables, broth, wine, seasoning and bay leaves to the veal. Bake, covered, at 325 degrees for 2 hours. Turn the veal. Bake, covered, for 15 minutes longer. Add the tomatoes. Bake, covered, for 15 minutes longer. Serve over brown and wild rice. Top with the Gremolata. **Yield: 8 servings.**

Gremolata

½ cup minced fresh parsley
2 tablespoons grated lemon zest
1 tablespoon minced garlic

Combine the parsley, lemon zest and garlic in a bowl and mix well. Chill, covered, until serving time.

Note: Osso Buco refers to the hole in the bone where the delicious marrow can be found. A very popular dish, this is flavorful and very tender.

VENISON ROAST

1 (5- to 6-pound) venison roast
½ cup red wine vinegar
1 fifth dry red wine
1 tablespoon salt
3 onions, sliced
⅔ cup milk
1 cup (or more) white wine
⅓ cup water
3 tablespoons sour cream, or 3 tablespoons currant jelly
2 to 3 tablespoons flour

Place the roast in a shallow dish. Combine the vinegar, red wine, salt and onions in a bowl and mix well. Pour over the roast. Marinate, covered, in the refrigerator for 1 to 2 days. Combine the milk, white wine and water in a bowl and mix well. Place the roast on a rack in a roasting pan; discard the marinade. Bake at 450 degrees for 15 minutes. Reduce the oven temperature to 350 degrees. Bake for 15 minutes per pound for medium rare or 20 minutes per pound for well done, basting with the white wine mixture every 15 to 20 minutes. Combine the remaining white wine mixture, pan drippings and sour cream in a bowl and mix well. Stir in the flour. Serve with the roast. **Yield: 10 to 12 servings.**

COUNTERTOP PASTA SAUCE WITH BRIE

4 ripe large tomatoes, chopped
3 garlic cloves, pressed
1 cup fresh basil, cut into small
    pieces

1 pound Brie cheese, rind removed
1 cup good-quality olive oil
Pepper to taste

Combine the tomatoes, garlic and basil in a large bowl and mix well.
Chop the cheese. Add the cheese, olive oil and pepper to the tomato
mixture and mix well. Let stand, covered with plastic wrap, for 2 hours
or longer to allow flavors to marry. Serve mixed with your favorite pasta
and sprinkled with freshly shredded Parmesan cheese. **Yield: 4 servings.**

Note: You may serve this pasta with salad and Italian bread for a tasty meal.

EASY VEGETARIAN PASTA SAUCE

1 can artichoke hearts, drained
    and chopped
1 (15- or 16-ounce) can Italian
    stewed tomatoes
1 can Great Northern beans

1 jar roasted red peppers, drained
    and chopped
½ jar capers or caperberries
1 teaspoon rosemary

Combine the artichoke hearts, undrained tomatoes, beans, red peppers,
capers and rosemary in a bowl and mix well. Serve with your favorite
pasta and sprinkle with shredded Parmesan cheese. **Yield: 4 servings.**

Note: Keep the ingredients for this dish on hand for a super-fast meal.

PERFECT MARINARA SAUCE

½ teaspoon hot red pepper flakes
2 teaspoons fennel seeds
1 medium yellow onion, chopped
3 tablespoons olive oil
4 large garlic cloves, pressed or minced
2 (28-ounce) cans organic peeled whole tomatoes, coarsely chopped
1 teaspoon onion salt
Black pepper to taste
2 bay leaves

Crush the red pepper flakes and fennel seeds in a clean coffee grinder or use a mortar and pestle. Sauté the onion in the olive oil in a 4-quart nonstick saucepan for 2 minutes. Add the pepper flakes and fennel seeds in center of pan. Cook for about 2 minutes. Add the garlic. Cook for 3 minutes, stirring constantly. Add the tomatoes, onion salt, black pepper and bay leaves and mix well. Simmer for 45 minutes, stirring occasionally. Remove and discard the bay leaves. Serve with angel hair pasta, crumbled goat cheese, grated Parmesan cheese or chopped fresh basil and oregano. **Yield: 2 quarts.**

From Tire Tubing To Water Skiing

A fun activity in the Big Basin at the McIntyres and Torrances was to attach a long rope to the boat and pull lots of kids in a train procession on black car or tractor inner tubes—not falling off was the challenge. Today, tubing behind boats is similar, but at a much, much faster speed.

Water skiing was by far the favorite of all boating activities and evolved from two wooden skis (often homemade) to fancy single skis called slaloms. You wanted to ski all day and sometimes skied the entire nine-mile length of the lake.

GRILLED LEMON PEPPER CHICKEN WITH GREMOLATA

¹/₄ cup fresh lemon juice
1 tablespoon coarsely ground pepper
Salt to taste
¹/₂ cup extra-virgin olive oil
3 whole boneless skinless chicken breasts, cut into halves
Gremolata

Combine the lemon juice, pepper and salt in a bowl and whisk to mix well. Add the olive oil in a stream, whisking constantly until emulsified. Pound the chicken ¹/₄ inch thick between pieces of plastic wrap using a rolling pin or meat mallet. Place the chicken in a sealable plastic bag. Add the lemon juice mixture. Marinate in the refrigerator for 30 minutes. Remove the chicken from the marinade, discarding the marinade. Arrange the chicken on a greased grill rack. Grill for 2 minutes per side or just until cooked through. Remove to a serving plate. Sprinkle with Gremolata. Garnish with lemon slices and thyme sprigs.
Yield: 6 servings.

GREMOLATA

1 tablespoon chopped fresh thyme
2 garlic cloves, minced
1 teaspoon freshly grated lemon zest

Combine the thyme, garlic and lemon zest in a bowl and mix well.

CHICKEN PICCATA

2 cups fresh soft bread crumbs
1/3 cup melted butter
1/2 cup grated Parmesan cheese
1/3 cup chopped fresh parsley
1 teaspoon garlic powder
6 boneless skinless chicken breasts, pounded
1/3 cup melted butter
2 to 3 garlic cloves, crushed
Juice of 1 lemon

Combine the bread crumbs, 1/3 cup butter, cheese, parsley and garlic powder in a bowl and mix well. Spoon about 1 tablespoon of the mixture onto each chicken breast, reserving the remaining mixture. Roll the chicken to enclose the filling. Arrange seam side down in a baking dish. Combine 1/3 cup butter, garlic and lemon juice in a bowl and mix well. Pour over the chicken. Sprinkle with the reserved bread crumb mixture. Bake at 375 degrees for 35 minutes. **Yield: 6 servings.**

CHICKEN MARBELLA

1 head garlic, puréed
¼ cup oregano
Salt and coarsely ground pepper to taste
½ cup red wine vinegar
½ cup olive oil
1 cup small pitted prunes
½ cup pitted Spanish olives
½ cup undrained capers
6 bay leaves
10 boneless chicken breasts
1 cup packed brown sugar
1 cup white wine
¼ cup finely chopped fresh parsley or cilantro
½ teaspoon instant mashed potatoes

Combine the garlic, oregano, salt, pepper, vinegar, olive oil, prunes, Spanish olives, capers and bay leaves in a bowl and mix well. Add the chicken; cover. Marinate in the refrigerator for 12 hours. You may marinate the chicken in a sealable plastic bag, turning the bag occasionally. Arrange the chicken in a single layer in a baking dish. Spoon the marinade over the chicken. Sprinkle with the brown sugar. Pour the wine over the top. Bake for 1 hour, basting frequently. Remove the chicken, prunes, olives and capers to a serving platter using a slotted spoon. Sprinkle with the parsley. Thicken the pan juices with the instant mashed potatoes. Pour into a sauce boat. Serve with the chicken and hot cooked brown rice or pasta. **Yield: 10 to 12 servings.**

Marinated Honey Lemon Chicken

¹/₂ cup lemon juice
¹/₄ cup vegetable oil
1 garlic clove, minced
2 teaspoons salt
1 teaspoon paprika
1 teaspoon pepper
1 tablespoon parsley
Sesame seeds
1 (2- to 3-pound) chicken, cut up, or 6 boneless chicken breasts
1 tablespoon honey

Combine the lemon juice, oil, garlic, salt, paprika, pepper, parsley and sesame seeds in a saucepan and mix well. Bring to a boil. Boil over low heat for 1 minute, stirring frequently. Let stand to cool. Place the marinade and chicken in a sealable plastic bag, turning to coat the chicken. Marinate in the refrigerator for 4 to 10 hours, turning occasionally. Remove the chicken from the marinade, reserving the marinade. Pour the reserved marinade into a saucepan. Add the honey and mix well. Cook until heated through, stirring frequently. Grill the chicken until cooked through, basting frequently with the marinade.
Yield: 4 servings.

Note: If you double this recipe, be sure to double the honey as it serves to cut the tartness.

TENDER CHICKEN OSKER

2 tablespoons olive oil or butter
1½ pounds chicken tenders, or 3 chicken breasts,
    cut into ½-inch strips
1 small jar pimentos, drained
1 small can mushrooms
¼ jar capers, drained
Salt and pepper to taste

Heat the olive oil in a skillet over medium-high heat. Cook the chicken, covered, in the hot oil until brown on both sides, turning once. Reduce the heat. Sprinkle the pimentos, undrained mushrooms and capers over the chicken. Season with salt and pepper. Simmer, covered, for 10 minutes or until the chicken is cooked through. Remove from the heat. Let stand, covered, for 5 minutes before serving. **Yield: 4 servings.**

Note: Serve with your favorite side dish, such as long grain and wild rice or risotto, and steamed asparagus.

Ro-Tel Chicken Pasta

5 chicken breasts, cooked and finely chopped
1 (10-ounce) can cream of mushroom soup
1 (10-ounce) can cream of chicken soup
1 (10-ounce) can Ro-Tel tomatoes with green chiles
1 (4-ounce) can sliced mushrooms, drained
12 ounces noodles or spaghetti
3 ounces cream cheese, softened
1 cup sour cream
1 cup (4 ounces) shredded Cheddar cheese

Combine the chicken, soups, tomatoes with green chiles and mushrooms in a bowl and mix well. Cook the noodles using the package directions; drain. Combine the hot pasta, cream cheese and sour cream in a bowl and mix well. Add the chicken mixture and mix well. Spoon into a 9×13-inch baking dish sprayed with nonstick cooking spray. Bake at 350 degrees for 40 minutes. Sprinkle with the Cheddar cheese. Bake for 20 minutes longer. Cut into squares. Serve with fruit salad and bread. **Yield: 6 to 8 servings.**

Note: Loaded with flavor, this dish is a real crowd pleaser. Reduced-fat soup works fine in this recipe.

CHICKEN SALSA WITH CHEESE GRITS SOUFFLÉ

2 (15-ounce) cans black beans,
    rinsed and drained
1 (15-ounce) can whole kernel
    corn, rinsed and drained
3 green onions, chopped
1 red or green bell pepper, chopped
6 plum tomatoes, chopped

1/4 cup chopped fresh cilantro
Salt and pepper to taste
1 (package) garlic- and herb-
    seasoned stuffing mix
3 whole boneless chicken breasts,
    cooked and chopped or sliced
Cheese Grits

Combine the beans, corn, green onions, bell pepper, tomatoes, cilantro, salt and pepper in a bowl and mix well. Prepare the stuffing mix using the package directions. Add the stuffing and chicken to the bean mixture and toss to mix. Spoon over servings of Cheese Grits. Serve with a fresh or congealed fruit salad. **Yield: 12 to 15 servings.**

CHEESE GRITS

1 cup quick grits
4 cups water
Salt (optional)
1/2 cup (1 stick) butter
1/2 teaspoon garlic powder, or
    1 teaspoon minced garlic

Hot red pepper sauce (optional)
16 ounces Velveeta cheese, chopped
1/4 cup each freshly grated
    Parmesan cheese and extra-
    sharp Cheddar cheese
2 eggs, beaten

Cook the grits in a large saucepan using the package directions using the water and salt. Add the butter, garlic powder, pepper sauce, Velveeta cheese, Parmesan cheese and Cheddar cheese and mix well. Cook over low heat until the Cheddar cheese is melted, stirring constantly. Add the eggs and mix well. Spoon into a 9×13-inch baking dish. Bake at 325 to 350 degrees for 25 minutes or until golden brown and set.

Note: You may make the salsa a day ahead, adding the tomatoes just before serving. For a shortcut, you may use precooked sliced chicken.

CHICKEN AND ARTICHOKE PIZZAS

5 small boneless skinless chicken breasts
1 container commercially prepared basil pesto
4 cups sliced fresh mushrooms
6 garlic cloves, chopped
1/4 cup (1/2 stick) butter
2 (14-ounce) cans artichoke bottoms, chopped
1 container commercially prepared basil pesto
2 (12-inch) baked pizza crusts
1 bunch green onions, chopped
1/2 cup pine nuts
1 cup crumbled feta cheese
2 cups (8 ounces) shredded mozzarella cheese

Place the chicken in a sealable plastic bag. Add 1 container pesto. Marinate in the refrigerator for 8 to 10 hours. Remove the chicken from the marinade and discard the marinade. Grill the chicken until cooked through. Let stand to cool slightly. Cut into thin slices. Sauté the mushrooms and garlic in the butter in a skillet until the mushrooms are tender. Stir in the artichokes. Remove from the heat. Spread 1 container pesto over the pizza crusts. Layer with the sliced chicken and artichoke mixture. Sprinkle with the green onions, pine nuts, feta cheese and mozzarella cheese. Bake at 350 degrees for 20 to 25 minutes or until the cheese is melted. **Yield: 16 slices.**

Note: You may add sautéed green and/or red bell peppers to add color. The chicken breasts are great by themselves right off the grill.

GRILLED TURKEY BURGERS

½ cup mayonnaise
3½ tablespoons chopped fresh basil
14 kalamata olives, pitted and finely chopped
1½ pounds ground turkey
2½ tablespoons chopped oil-pack sun-dried tomatoes
Salt and pepper to taste
5 or 6 sesame seed buns
Lettuce

Combine the mayonnaise and basil in a bowl and mix well. Set aside.
Combine the olives, ground turkey, sun-dried tomatoes, salt and pepper
in a large bowl and mix well. Shape into five or six 1-inch patties,
handling the mixture as little as possible. Grill for 4½ minutes per side
or until well done. You may cook the burgers in a well-seasoned cast-
iron skillet or in a ridged grill pan. Toast the buns. Remove the burgers
to the buns. Serve the burgers with lettuce and the basil mayonnaise
mixture. **Yield: 5 or 6 burgers.**

SMOTHERED QUAIL OR DOVE

8 quail or dove, split
Salt and black pepper to taste
Cayenne pepper to taste
Flour
1/2 cup olive oil
2 onions, chopped
1/2 green bell pepper, chopped
3 ribs celery
1/2 cup chicken broth
Timesaving Brown Roux in the Microwave (page 132)

Season the quail with salt, black pepper and cayenne pepper. Dust with flour. Brown the quail in the olive oil in a skillet. Add the onions, bell pepper and celery. Cook just until the vegetables are tender-crisp, stirring frequently. Add the broth. Cook for 30 minutes or until the quail is tender. Remove the quail to a plate. Add the roux to the pan drippings and mix well. Return the quail to the skillet. Spoon the sauce over the top and serve. **Yield: 4 servings.**

GINGER-CRUSTED GROUPER WITH ORANGE JALAPEÑO SAUCE

1 cup seasoned bread crumbs
3 ounces candied ginger
1 tablespoon lemon juice
4 (8-ounce) grouper fillets
¼ cup (½ stick) butter, softened
1 cup orange juice
16 slices jalapeño chiles
½ cup (1 stick) butter, cut into 8 pieces

Combine the bread crumbs and ginger in a food processor. Process until mixed. Add the lemon juice and mix well. Spread the mixture on a plate. Press the fillets top side down onto the bread crumb mixture. Heat 2 tablespoons of the butter in a skillet over medium-low heat. Place the fillets breaded side down in the butter. Cook for 4 minutes per side or until cooked through. Repeat the cooking procedure using 2 tablespoons butter and the remaining fillets. Bring the orange juice almost to a boil in a small skillet. Add the jalapeño chiles. Remove from the heat. Remove and reserve the jalapeño chiles. Add ¹/₂ cup butter to the orange juice. Swirl until the butter is melted. Pour equal portions of the butter mixture onto each of 4 individual serving plates. Place a fillet on each plate, arranging 4 reserved jalapeño chiles on each plate. Serve immediately.
Yield: 4 servings.

From McKinnon's Louisiane Restaurant, Atlanta, Georgia,
Bill Glendinning, chef

Onion-Crusted Salmon

1 large can onion rings
2 sprigs of dill weed

4 (4- to 6-ounce) salmon fillets
1½ cups buttermilk

Process the onion rings and dill weed in a food processor or blender until crushed. Place the salmon in the buttermilk in a bowl. Marinate in the refrigerator for 30 minutes. Press the onion ring mixture onto the surface of the salmon. Arrange in a baking dish sprayed with nonstick cooking spray. Bake at 375 degrees for 25 minutes or until cooked to the desired degree of doneness. **Yield: 4 servings.**

Fifteen-Minute Grilled Salmon with Angel Hair

1 (10-ounce) salmon fillet
9 ounces refrigerated angel hair
    pasta
¼ cup drained capers

¼ cup grated Parmesan cheese
Freshly cracked pepper to taste
¼ cup olive oil

Grill the salmon until it flakes easily. Cook the pasta in boiling water in a saucepan until al dente; drain. Rinse and drain again. Place the pasta in a bowl. Flake the salmon into the pasta. Add the remaining ingredients and mix well. Serve immediately with buttered bread and a green salad. **Yield: 3 servings.**

Note: You may use smoked salmon in this recipe. Do not prepare ahead of time. The dish must be served immediately. You will not believe how good it is.

SALMON CROQUETTES

1 (15-ounce) can red salmon,
    drained
1 egg, beaten
1 teaspoon seasoned salt
1 tablespoon lemon juice
1/4 teaspoon pepper

1 1/2 tablespoons parsley
1 tablespoon onion flakes
1/4 cup mayonnaise
1 package herb-seasoned
    stuffing mix
Olive oil

Combine the salmon, egg, seasoned salt, lemon juice, pepper, parsley, onion flakes and mayonnaise in a bowl and mix well. Shape into 5 patties. Coat with the stuffing mix. Heat a small amount of olive oil in a skillet over medium heat. Cook the patties in the hot oil until brown, turning once. Serve with Tartar Sauce (page 137). **Yield: 5 servings.**

Note: These croquettes may be wrapped in plastic wrap and frozen. You may want to add more seasonings to this recipe.

FISH AND POTATO CASSEROLE

1/4 cup vegetable oil
4 garlic cloves, crushed
2 teaspoons salt
1/2 teaspoon cumin
Freshly ground pepper to taste
1/4 cup fresh lemon juice

4 tilapia fillets
2 Idaho potatoes, peeled and very
    thinly sliced
2 large carrots, julienned
3 tomatoes, cut into 1/4-inch slices

Combine the oil, garlic, salt, cumin, pepper and lemon juice in a bowl and mix well. Pour into a 9×13-inch baking dish. Arrange the fillets in the dish. Layer the potatoes, carrots and tomatoes on top of the fish. Cover with foil. Bake at 375 degrees for 30 minutes or until the potatoes are tender. Serve in pasta bowls with the pan juices. **Yield: 4 servings.**

Fish Tacos "A Texas Thing"

5 tilapia fillets
Flour
Olive oil
3 Roma tomatoes, chopped
½ cup guacamole
1 jar corn salsa or salsa
2 cups finely shredded cabbage
½ cup reduced-fat sour cream
1 cup (4 ounces) shredded mild Cheddar cheese
1 cup (4 ounces) shredded Pepper Jack cheese
6 whole wheat tortillas

Cut the fish lengthwise into 1¹/₂-inch strips. Coat with flour. Cook in a small amount of olive oil in a skillet until the fish is brown and flakes easily, turning once. Remove to a serving dish. Place the tomatoes, guacamole, corn salsa, cabbage, sour cream, Cheddar cheese and Pepper Jack cheese in individual bowls. Wrap the tortillas in foil and warm in a slow oven. You may wrap 2 tortillas at a time in paper towels and microwave for 20 seconds. Serve with the fish and taco fixings.
Yield: 4 servings.

Note: Mango Texas Margaritas (page 31) are a must with these tacos.

Pawleys Island Crab Cakes

1 pound white lump crab meat, drained and flaked
1 egg, beaten
1 teaspoon seasoned salt
2 to 3 teaspoons lemon juice
Pepper to taste
1½ tablespoons chopped fresh parsley
¼ cup Duke's Mayonnaise
1 to 2 sleeves butter crackers, crushed
Olive oil

Combine the crab meat, egg, seasoned salt, lemon juice, pepper, parsley and mayonnaise in a bowl and mix well. Shape into 5 patties. Coat with the cracker crumbs. Chill, covered, until serving time. Cook in a small amount of olive oil in a skillet over medium-high heat until brown, turning once. Serve with rémoulade sauce if desired. **Yield: 5 crab cakes.**

Note: These crab cakes are a number one seller at the Christ Church Bazaar. They freeze well uncooked and wrapped in plastic wrap. Partially thaw the frozen crab cakes before cooking. You may want to adjust the seasonings.

Vacation Pizza

1 red, green or yellow bell pepper, chopped
¼ cup chopped onion
1 tablespoon olive oil
1 pound fresh or thawed frozen small shrimp,
    peeled and deveined
1½ teaspoons Old Bay seasoning
Pizza or marinara sauce (optional)
1 (12-inch) baked pizza crust
2 cups fresh spinach
½ to 1 teaspoon cumin
¼ teaspoon cayenne pepper
1½ cups (6 ounces) shredded Monterey Jack cheese

Sauté the bell pepper and onion in the olive oil in a skillet until tender.
Place the shrimp in a bowl. Add the Old Bay seasoning and toss to coat.
Spread pizza sauce over the pizza crust. Arrange the spinach on top of
the pizza sauce. Sprinkle with the cumin and cayenne pepper. Layer
with the shrimp mixture, bell pepper mixture and cheese. Bake at
400 degrees for 25 minutes. **Yield: 3 servings.**

Note: You may use a combination of red, green and yellow bell peppers. Using
thawed frozen shrimp makes this a quick recipe to prepare. Small shrimp are
recommended because they cook faster than large shrimp.

Shortcut Shrimp Creole with Cheese Rice

2 jars Classico Italian Sausage Pasta Sauce
1 can Progresso Hearty Tomato Soup
2 teaspoons McCormick Cajun Seasoning, or to taste
2 pounds frozen cooked shrimp
1 pound kielbasa, sliced and sautéed
4 cups water
2 cups rice
2 teaspoons salt
1 onion, chopped
1 cup (4 ounces) shredded sharp Cheddar cheese

Combine the pasta sauce, soup and Cajun seasoning in a stockpot. Simmer for 15 minutes, stirring occasionally. Add the shrimp and kielbasa and mix well. Cook for 15 minutes, stirring occasionally. Bring the water to a boil in a saucepan. Add the rice, salt and onion and mix well. Bring to a boil; cover. Reduce the heat to low. Cook for 20 minutes. Stir in the cheese. Spoon onto individual serving plates. Spoon the shrimp mixture over the rice. Serve immediately. **Yield: 8 servings.**

Note: This short version of Shrimp Creole is just as good as the long version.

DOUBLE-BATCH SHRIMP FLORENTINE

4 (10-ounce) packages frozen chopped spinach,
    thawed and drained
3 pounds shrimp, peeled and deveined
1/2 cup grated Parmesan cheese
1/2 cup (1 stick) butter or margarine
1/2 cup flour
3 cups milk
1 cup dry white wine
1/2 cup chopped scallions
Salt and pepper to taste
Paprika to taste
2 cups (8 ounces) shredded Cheddar cheese

Line two 9-inch pie plates with heavy-duty foil. Combine the spinach,
shrimp and Parmesan cheese in a bowl and mix well. Spread half the
mixture in each prepared pie plate. Melt the butter in a saucepan. Stir in
the flour. Add the milk, wine and scallions gradually, stirring constantly.
Cook over low heat until thickened and bubbly, stirring constantly. Add
salt, pepper and paprika and mix well. Pour over the spinach mixture.
Sprinkle with the Cheddar cheese. Bake at 350 degrees for 35 minutes or
until bubbly. You may freeze 1 batch for future use. After the mixture
freezes, remove from the pie plate and wrap in foil to store in the freezer.
Unwrap the frozen mixture, place in a foil-lined pie plate and bake at
350 degrees for 1 hour or until bubbly. **Yield: 8 servings.**

Baked Stuffed Shrimp

2 pounds jumbo shrimp (about 16 to 20 count per pound)
½ cup chopped green onions
4 garlic cloves, minced
Olive oil
1 tablespoon Worcestershire sauce
¼ cup lemon juice
2 tablespoons dry sherry or sake
½ cup (1 stick) butter, softened
2 tablespoons Dijon mustard
1½ cups seasoned bread crumbs

Peel and butterfly the shrimp. Sauté the green onions and garlic in a small amount of olive oil in a skillet until tender. Add the Worcestershire sauce, lemon juice, sherry, butter and Dijon mustard and mix well. Add enough of the bread crumbs to make the consistency of a paste. Arrange the shrimp in a baking pan with the tails pointed up. Shape the bread crumb mixture into 1-inch balls (the size of a ping pong ball). Place 1 stuffing ball on each shrimp. Spray with nonstick cooking spray. Bake at 350 degrees for 30 minutes. **Yield: 6 servings.**

Shrimp and Feta Cheese with Vermicelli

1 pound medium shrimp, peeled and deveined
2 tablespoons olive oil
2/3 cup crumbled feta cheese
2 tablespoons olive oil
1/2 teaspoon crushed garlic
1 (15-ounce) can tomato wedges
1/4 cup white wine
3/4 teaspoon basil
1/2 teaspoon oregano
1/4 teaspoon salt
1/4 teaspoon pepper
8 ounces vermicelli, cooked and drained

Sauté the shrimp in 2 tablespoons olive oil in a skillet for 1 to 2 minutes or until the shrimp turn pink. Arrange in an 8×10-inch baking dish. Sprinkle with the cheese. Add 2 tablespoons olive oil to the skillet. Reduce the heat to low. Sauté the garlic in the olive oil until tender. Add the undrained tomatoes. Cook for 1 minute. Stir in the wine, basil, oregano, salt and pepper. Simmer for 10 minutes. Spoon over the shrimp. Bake at 400 degrees for 10 minutes. Serve over the vermicelli. **Yield: 3 to 4 servings.**

Note: You may add 3 or 4 hot red pepper flakes to the shrimp while sautéing. These are very hot so a little goes a long way to spice up your food.

From Square Dancing To the Vegetable Men

One of the most memorable and fun off-the-lake entertainments on
Saturday nights was the Square Dance at Mountain City, held in the
Mountain City Playhouse. The music was lively with a honky-tonk
piano, fiddle, and guitars. Here residents from the lake and all parts
of Rabun County could swing their partners high and low to the
commands of the caller: "Circle up four, swing your partner, do-si-do,
shoot the star, eight hands over, and bird in the cage." Square dances
were alternated with country waltzes and buck dancing. Buck dancing
was a form of clogging only done by the men or "bucks." That custom
changed to include all ages and women in the 1960s. Now clogging
is a beloved tradition at lake gatherings when the bluegrass music
starts playing.

Another common sight on the lake road in the olden days was the
Vegetable Men. Mr. Stubblefield and Mr. Harrines brought wonderful
fresh vegetables to the lake residents in their pickups with the scale
swinging on the back. Occasionally, the famous Goat Man, Ches
McCartney, would be seen traveling across Rabun County with his
heavily laden wagon and herd of goats.

LEMON ARTICHOKE HEARTS

2 (14-ounce) cans artichoke hearts, drained
3/4 cup minced onion
2 garlic cloves, crushed
2 tablespoons butter
1 1/2 cups chicken broth
3 tablespoons lemon juice
1 teaspoon oregano
1 teaspoon salt

Cut the artichoke hearts into halves. Sauté the onion and garlic in the butter in a skillet until tender but not brown. Add the artichokes, broth, lemon juice, oregano and salt and mix well. Simmer for 10 minutes or until heated through, stirring occasionally. **Yield: 4 to 6 servings.**

Note: This artichoke dish is great with steak.

Go with Anything Beans

4 medium onions, chopped
¼ cup corn oil
6 to 8 slices bacon, crisp-cooked and crumbled
2 tablespoons prepared mustard
½ cup apple cider vinegar
½ cup packed brown sugar
1 (14-ounce) can lima beans, drained
1 (14-ounce) can Great Northern beans, drained
1 (14-ounce) can kidney beans, drained
2 (14-ounce) cans pork and beans

Sauté the onions in the corn oil in a skillet. Stir in the bacon, prepared mustard, vinegar and brown sugar. Combine the lima beans, Great Northern beans, kidney beans, pork and beans and onion mixture in a bowl and mix well. Spoon into a 3-quart baking dish. Bake at 350 degrees for 1 hour. **Yield: 10 to 15 servings.**

Note: You may brown 8 ounces ground beef with the onions for a one-dish meal.

Broccoli Tomato Casserole

12 cherry tomatoes
¼ teaspoon salt
⅛ teaspoon pepper
1 package frozen chopped broccoli, thawed and drained
1 cup (4 ounces) shredded sharp Cheddar cheese
1 small onion, grated
3 tablespoons margarine, cut into small pieces

Cut the tomatoes into halves. Place cut side up in an 8-inch round baking dish. Sprinkle with the salt and pepper. Combine the broccoli, cheese and onion in a bowl and mix well. Spoon over the tomatoes. Dot with the margarine. Cover tightly with foil. Bake at 350 degrees for 20 minutes. **Yield: 6 servings.**

Note: You may grill this casserole in a foil packet over medium heat for 20 minutes.

Ancient Sweet-and-Sour Red Cabbage

1 medium red cabbage
1 tart apple, chopped (Rome preferred)
1 tablespoon shortening
³/4 cup apple cider vinegar
¹/2 cup apple juice or cider
³/4 cup sugar
1 teaspoon salt
¹/2 teaspoon pepper
¹/2 teaspoon celery seeds

Cut or shred the cabbage into tiny pieces. Combine the cabbage, apple, shortening, vinegar, juice, sugar, salt, pepper and celery seeds in a 3-quart saucepan. Cook for 1¹/2 hours or until the cabbage is very tender, adding additional sugar or vinegar if needed. **Yield: 8 to 10 servings.**

Note: This recipe is more than 100 years old.

CREAMED CORN IN THE MICROWAVE

6 medium ears of sweet corn
¹/₄ cup (¹/₂ stick) butter or margarine
¹/₄ cup water
1 teaspoon sugar
¹/₂ cup half-and-half
2 teaspoons cornstarch
¹/₂ teaspoon salt
¹/₂ teaspoon pepper

Cut the corn from the cob, scraping the cobs. Place the butter in a 2-quart microwave-safe dish. Microwave on High for 1 minute or until melted. Stir in the corn, water and sugar. Microwave, covered with plastic wrap, on High for 3 minutes. Stir and turn the dish a half turn. Microwave, covered, for 5 to 7 minutes or until the corn is tender. Combine the half-and-half, cornstarch, salt and pepper in a bowl. Whisk until the cornstarch is dissolved. Add to the corn mixture and mix well. Microwave, covered, on High for 2¹/₂ minutes or until thickened, stirring at 1-minute intervals. **Yield: 4 to 6 servings.**

South Georgia Baked Onions

4 Vidalia onions
4 tablespoons bourbon
2 tablespoons butter
4 teaspoons brown sugar

Cut off the bottom of the onions and remove the skins. Place on individual pieces of foil. Pour 1 tablespoon bourbon over each onion. Top each onion with $1/2$ tablespoon butter and 1 teaspoon brown sugar. Fold the foil to enclose the onions. Bake at 350 degrees for 45 minutes. **Yield: 4 servings.**

Note: Baked onions are great with steak or pork.

Sweet Vidalia Onion Scallop

¹/₄ cup (¹/₂ stick) butter or margarine
3 medium Vidalia onions, sliced
¹/₄ cup chopped green bell pepper
2 tablespoons chopped pimento
1 cup (4 ounces) shredded Swiss cheese
1 cup cracker crumbs
2 eggs
³/₄ cup half-and-half
Salt and pepper to taste
2 tablespoons butter or margarine, melted

Melt ¹/₄ cup butter in a heavy skillet over medium heat. Add the onions and green pepper. Cook until tender, stirring constantly. Stir in the pimento. Spoon half the onion mixture into a greased 8×8-inch baking dish. Sprinkle with half the cheese and half the cracker crumbs. Repeat layers of onion mixture and cheese. Beat the eggs in a medium bowl. Add the half-and-half, salt and pepper and mix well. Pour over the layers. Sprinkle with the remaining cracker crumbs. Drizzle with the melted butter. Bake at 350 degrees for 25 minutes. **Yield: 6 servings.**

Red Potatoes with Vinegar and Sea Salt

3 pounds new potatoes, chopped
2¹/₂ tablespoons tarragon vinegar or cider vinegar
Flaked or fine sea salt to taste
1¹/₂ tablespoons good-quality extra-virgin olive oil

Combine the potatoes and enough cold water to cover in a saucepan.
Bring to a boil. Simmer for 10 minutes or just until tender; drain. Rinse
briefly with cold water; drain well. Combine the warm potatoes, vinegar
and sea salt in a bowl and mix well. Cool to room temperature. Add the
olive oil and toss to mix. Serve immediately. **Yield: 8 servings.**

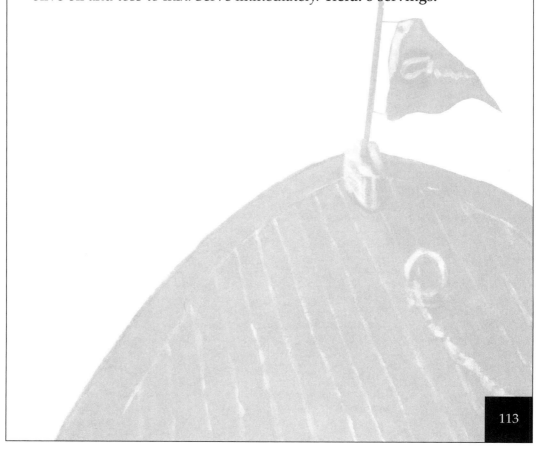

ROASTED SWEET POTATOES

1 tablespoon plus 1 teaspoon olive oil
4 unpeeled garlic cloves
2 sprigs of fresh rosemary, or ½ teaspoon dried rosemary
1 pound peeled sweet potatoes, cut into ¾-inch pieces
¼ cup chicken broth
½ teaspoon salt

Combine the olive oil, garlic and rosemary in a 9×9-inch baking dish.
Bake at 350 degrees for 7 minutes or until the olive oil is hot. Add the
sweet potatoes and stir to coat. Roast for 30 minutes, turning occasionally.
Add the broth. Bake for 15 minutes or until the sweet potatoes are
brown and cooked through, turning occasionally. Remove and discard
the garlic and rosemary. Sprinkle with the salt. **Yield: 4 servings.**

Note: You may substitute other root vegetables, such as rutabagas, for some of
the sweet potatoes. These are great with chicken.

Steamed Spinach with Roasted Garlic

2 pounds spinach, stems removed
2 tablespoons water
1 to 2 tablespoons olive oil
4 large garlic cloves, roasted and coarsely chopped
Grated Parmesan cheese (optional)

Steam the spinach in the water in a large covered saucepan over medium-high heat for 3 to 5 minutes. Drain the spinach, squeezing out the excess water. Combine the spinach, olive oil and garlic in a bowl and toss to mix. Spoon into a $1^1/2$-quart baking dish. Bake, covered, at 325 degrees for 10 minutes or until heated through. Sprinkle with cheese. **Yield: 4 servings.**

Note: To roast the garlic, cut the tips off the unpeeled garlic cloves. Place the cloves in a clay roaster or foil. Roast at 350 to 400 degrees for 1 hour or until the skins begin to brown. Let stand to cool. Squeeze out the garlic.

Summer Squash Casserole in Potato Crust

3 cups frozen shredded hash brown potatoes, thawed
1/4 cup chopped onion
1/4 cup grated Parmesan cheese
1 egg, beaten
2 medium zucchini
1 garlic clove, minced
2 tablespoons butter
3 eggs, beaten
1/2 cup milk
1/2 cup (2 ounces) shredded Cheddar cheese
1/2 teaspoon oregano
Salt and pepper to taste

Combine the potatoes, onion, Parmesan cheese and 1 egg in a bowl and mix well. Spread over the bottom and up the side of a pie plate or baking dish. Bake at 350 degrees for 30 to 40 minutes or until golden brown. Maintain the oven temperature. Let the crust stand to cool slightly. Sauté the zucchini and garlic in the butter in a skillet until tender. Spread evenly over the crust. Combine 3 eggs, the milk, Cheddar cheese, oregano, salt and pepper in a bowl and mix well. Pour over the zucchini mixture. Bake for 35 minutes or until set. **Yield: 6 to 8 servings.**

Summer Squash with a Twist

6 medium yellow squash, ends trimmed
1/2 cup chopped green onions
2 small tomatillos, husked and chopped
3/4 cup shredded Monterey Jack cheese
5 slices bacon, crisp-cooked and crumbled
1/4 cup bread crumbs
2 to 3 tablespoons melted butter

Steam the squash until tender; drain. Let stand to cool for 10 to 15 minutes. Cut lengthwise into halves. Scoop out the pulp, removing the pulp to a bowl and reserving the shells. Add the green onions, tomatillos, cheese and bacon to the squash pulp and mix well. Fill the reserved shells with the mixture. Arrange in a 9×13-inch baking dish. Sprinkle with the bread crumbs. Drizzle with the butter. Bake at 350 degrees for 25 to 30 minutes. You may bake the squash ahead of time, refrigerate, covered, and reheat before serving. **Yield: 6 servings.**

TOMATO PIE

4 to 6 tomatoes
1 refrigerated pie pastry
1/2 cup (2 ounces) shredded mozzarella cheese or
*   crumbled blue or feta cheese*
1/3 to 1/2 cup mayonnaise
1/3 to 1/2 cup sour cream
1 bunch fresh basil, chopped
Salt and pepper to taste
Grated Parmesan cheese (optional)

Cut the unpeeled tomatoes into thick slices. Drain on paper towels for 5 minutes. Fit the pie pastry into a pie plate. Bake for 10 minutes using the package directions. Combine the mozzarella cheese, mayonnaise, sour cream, basil, salt and pepper in a bowl and mix well. Layer the tomatoes and cheese mixture 1/2 at a time in the piecrust, ending with the cheese mixture. Bake at 350 degrees for 30 minutes. Sprinkle with the Parmesan cheese. Let stand for 5 to 10 minutes before serving.
Yield: 4 to 6 servings.

STUFFED TOMATOES

8 medium tomatoes
2 (10-ounce) packages frozen chopped spinach
1 cup chopped onion
¼ cup (½ stick) butter
1 cup sour cream
½ cup grated Parmesan cheese
1 (14-ounce) can artichokes, drained and chopped

Cut the tops off of the tomatoes. Scoop out the pulp, reserving the shells.
Cook the spinach using the package directions; drain well. Sauté the
onion in the butter in a skillet until tender. Combine the spinach, sautéed
onion, sour cream, cheese and artichokes in a bowl and mix well. Spoon
into the tomatoes. Bake at 350 degrees for 25 minutes. **Yield: 8 servings.**

Turnip Greens Casserole Style

2 (16-ounce) cans chopped turnip greens, drained
1 teaspoon sugar
1 (10-ounce) can cream of mushroom soup
½ cup mayonnaise
¼ cup wine vinegar
1 teaspoon (heaping) prepared horseradish
2 eggs, beaten
Butter cracker crumbs or buttered bread crumbs
Paprika

Combine the turnip greens, sugar, soup, mayonnaise, vinegar, horseradish and eggs in a bowl and mix well. Spoon into a 2-quart baking dish. Top with cracker crumbs. Sprinkle with paprika. Bake at 350 degrees for 1 hour. **Yield: 6 to 8 servings.**

Note: This casserole is easy to multiply for a large crowd. It is a good do-ahead New Year's Day dish; serve with black-eyed peas and pork tenderloin or ham.

Zucchini, Squash and Tomato Casserole

1½ pounds zucchini, cut into ⅜-inch slices
1½ pounds yellow squash, cut into ⅜-inch slices
Salt to taste
¼ cup (½ stick) butter, cut into small pieces
1 tablespoon Cavender's Greek Seasoning
1 medium Vidalia onion, chopped
½ cup half-and-half
2 eggs, beaten
1 to 2 cups (4 to 8 ounces) shredded sharp Cheddar cheese
½ cup coarse bread crumbs
¼ cup (½ stick) butter, cut into small pieces
½ cup grated Parmesan cheese
9 grape tomatoes

Combine the zucchini, yellow squash and enough salted water to cover in a saucepan. Cook for 10 minutes or just until tender; drain. Place in a 9×13-inch baking dish. Dot with ¼ cup butter. Sprinkle with the Greek seasoning and onion. Combine the half-and-half and eggs in a bowl and mix well. Pour over the onion mixture. Layer with the Cheddar cheese, bread crumbs, ¼ cup butter and Parmesan cheese. Arrange the grape tomatoes on top so that each serving will have a tomato. Bake at 450 degrees for 20 minutes. **Yield: 9 servings.**

Vegetable Casserole

2 (14-ounce) cans French-style green beans, drained
1 (14-ounce) can Shoe Peg corn, drained
1 (14-ounce) can cream of celery soup
1 cup sour cream
1/2 teaspoon dill weed
1/2 cup chopped celery
1/2 cup chopped green bell pepper
1/2 cup chopped onion
1/2 cup (2 ounces) shredded sharp Cheddar cheese
1 (2-ounce) jar pimentos
Salt and pepper to taste
1 sleeve butter crackers, crushed
1/2 cup slivered almonds
1/4 cup (1/2 stick) butter, melted

Combine the green beans, corn, soup, sour cream, dill weed, celery, bell pepper, onion, cheese, pimentos, salt and pepper in a bowl and mix well. Spoon into a 9×13-inch baking dish. Combine the cracker crumbs, almonds and butter in a bowl and mix well. Sprinkle over the green bean mixture. Bake at 350 degrees for 30 minutes.
Yield: 10 to 12 servings.

ROASTED VEGETABLES

Olive oil
1/4 cup fresh rosemary leaves
Salt and pepper to taste
5 pounds red potatoes,
    cut into halves
1 to 2 pounds green beans,
    trimmed
1 bunch carrots, peeled and cut
    lengthwise into halves
2 onions, sliced

2 red bell peppers, cut into
    1-inch strips
1/4 cup balsamic vinegar
1 tablespoon Dijon mustard
1 garlic clove, minced
1 tablespoon minced fresh parsley
1 tablespoon fresh rosemary leaves
1/2 cup olive oil
Kalamata olives (optional)
Tomatoes (optional)

Brush a baking sheet with a small amount of olive oil. Combine 1/4 cup rosemary, salt and pepper in a bowl and mix well. Press the cut surface of the potatoes into the rosemary mixture. Arrange cut side down on the prepared baking sheet. Brush with olive oil. Arrange the green beans, carrots, onions and bell peppers in a 9×13-inch baking dish. Brush lightly with olive oil. Sprinkle with salt and pepper. Bake the potatoes and green bean mixture at 400 degrees for 30 minutes. Combine the potatoes and green bean mixture in a bowl and mix well. Combine the vinegar and Dijon mustard in a bowl and whisk to mix. Add the garlic, parsley and 1 tablespoon rosemary and mix well. Add 1/2 cup olive oil in a fine stream, whisking constantly. Drizzle over the roasted vegetables. Add the kalamata olives and tomatoes and toss to mix. **Yield: 8 to 10 servings.**

Garlicky Fried Potato Spears

3 pounds large russet potatoes
2 quarts vegetable oil for frying
¼ cup finely chopped garlic
¼ cup finely chopped fresh parsley
2 teaspoons kosher salt
2 teaspoons freshly ground pepper

Scrub the potatoes thoroughly in cold water, removing any visible eyes or dark spots. Cut each potato lengthwise into 6 to 8 large spears. Combine the potato spears with enough cold water to cover in a saucepan.

Heat the oil in a large saucepan or an electric deep-fryer to 300 degrees. Remove half the potatoes from the water and drain. Deep-fry for 5 minutes in the hot oil. Remove from the oil and drain. Arrange the spears in a single layer on a baking sheet lined with paper towels and refrigerate. Repeat the process with the remaining potatoes. Potatoes must be completely chilled before proceeding. This step can be done up to 12 hours in advance.

Reheat the oil to 370 degrees. Deep-fry several potato spears at a time for 2 minutes or until crisp and golden in color. Remove the potatoes from the oil, shaking off any excess oil.

Place the hot potatoes in a large bowl. Sprinkle with the garlic, parsley, kosher salt and pepper. Toss until evenly coated. Transfer to a serving platter and serve immediately. **Yield: 6 servings.**

From LongHorn Steakhouse

Vegetables in a Pouch

1 medium onion, sliced
1 green bell pepper, sliced
1 yellow bell pepper, sliced
1 red bell pepper, sliced
8 small Yukon gold potatoes, sliced
1 tablespoon Dijon mustard
1 tablespoon minced garlic
½ cup olive oil
1 tablespoon chopped fresh rosemary
Salt and pepper to taste

Combine the onion, bell peppers and potatoes in a bowl. Combine the Dijon mustard, garlic, olive oil, rosemary, salt and pepper in a bowl and whisk to mix well. Pour over the vegetables and toss to coat. Spoon onto a large piece of foil. Fold to enclose the vegetables. Bake at 350 degrees for 20 minutes. You may grill the vegetables in the foil packet. **Yield: 8 servings.**

Lemon Rice

2 tablespoons butter
1 tablespoon vegetable oil
2 garlic cloves, crushed
1 cup long grain rice
1 3/4 cups chicken broth
1/4 cup lemon juice
1 1/2 teaspoons grated lemon zest
1/2 teaspoon salt
1/4 teaspoon pepper

Heat the butter and oil in a baking dish over medium-high heat. Stir in the garlic. Cook until tender, stirring constantly. Add the rice and stir until coated. Add the broth, lemon juice, lemon zest, salt and pepper and mix well. Bring to a boil; cover. Bake at 350 degrees for 25 to 30 minutes or until the liquid is absorbed and the rice is tender. Garnish with chopped fresh parsley, additional lemon zest and/or toasted pine nuts or almonds. **Yield: 4 servings.**

*Note: Orange juice and zest may be used to make **Orange Rice,** which is great with fish or chicken.*

Señor's Mexican Rice

2 cups cooked rice
2 cups sour cream
8 ounces Cheddar cheese, shredded
2 (6-ounce) cans chopped green chiles
Grated Parmesan cheese to taste
Chopped butter to taste

Combine the rice and sour cream in a bowl and mix well. Spoon half the mixture into a medium baking dish. Layer with the Cheddar cheese, green chiles and remaining rice mixture. Sprinkle with the Parmesan cheese and butter. Bake at 350 degrees for 30 minutes. **Yield: 6 to 8 servings.**

Note: Always a hit, this rice dish freezes well.

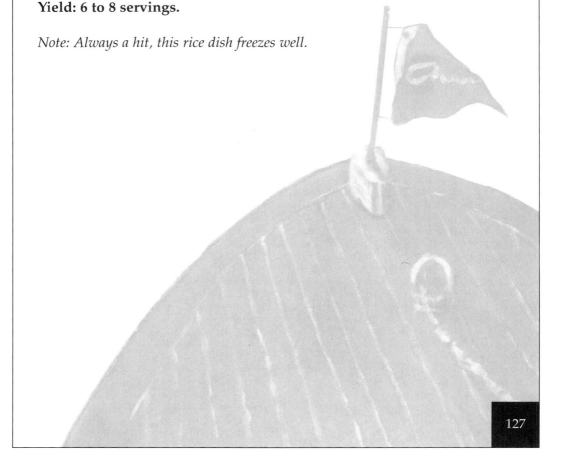

Hot Baked Fruit

1 (1-pound) package small pitted prunes
1 (11-ounce) package dried apricots
1 (13-ounce) can juice-pack pineapple chunks
1 (21-ounce) can cherry pie filling
1/4 cup dry sherry
1 1/2 cups water

Combine the prunes, apricots, undrained pineapple, pie filling, sherry and water in a bowl and mix well. Spoon into a baking dish. Bake at 350 degrees for 1 1/2 hours. **Yield: 10 servings.**

Note: Baked fruit is great with ham at Thanksgiving.

TRIPLE-FRUIT SALSA

1 cup chopped fresh pineapple or undrained canned pineapple tidbits
1 cup chopped fresh papaya or mango
1 kiwifruit, chopped
³/₄ cup chopped red bell pepper
3 tablespoons minced fresh cilantro
1¹/₂ tablespoons white wine vinegar
¹/₄ to ¹/₂ teaspoon hot red pepper flakes

Combine the pineapple, papaya, kiwifruit, bell pepper, cilantro, vinegar and pepper flakes in a bowl and toss gently. Chill, covered, for up to 8 hours. Let stand at room temperature before serving. Serve with a slotted spoon. **Yield: 2 cups.**

Note: Beware, red pepper flakes are very hot.

HOT PEPPER AND ORANGE PRESERVES

½ navel orange
1 to 1½ fresh hot red chile peppers
1 cup sugar
¼ cup water
2 tablespoons fresh lemon juice

Cut the orange into 4 wedges. Remove the seeds. Remove the stem and seeds carefully from the chile peppers. Cut into quarters. Combine the orange and chile peppers in a food processor. Process until puréed. Transfer to a 2-quart microwave-safe dish. Add the sugar, water and lemon juice and mix well. Microwave on High for 2 minutes; stir. Microwave for 4 to 5 minutes or until thickened. Let stand to cool. Chill, covered, until serving time. Serve with biscuits or corn bread. **Yield: 1⅓ cups.**

Note: Wear gloves when working with the chile peppers, or wash hands very thoroughly afterwards.

Garlic Pickles

1 (1-quart) jar sliced dill pickles, drained (not kosher)
1/2 teaspoon alum
1 cup cider vinegar
1 cup water
2 cups sugar
2 tablespoons mixed pickling spices
1/2 teaspoon alum
3 garlic cloves, cut into halves

Combine the pickles, 1/2 teaspoon alum and enough water to cover in a nonreactive bowl. Let stand, covered, overnight. Drain and rinse the pickles. Combine the vinegar, 1 cup water, sugar and pickling spices in a saucepan. Cook for 5 to 7 minutes or until the sugar is dissolved, stirring constantly. Add 1/2 teaspoon alum and mix well. Place 2 garlic halves in the pickle jar or a 1-quart canning jar. Add half the pickles. Layer with 2 garlic halves, the remaining pickles and the remaining garlic halves. Place a teaspoon in the jar to absorb the heat. Pour the vinegar mixture over the pickles. Remove the spoon; cover. Let stand to cool. Chill for 5 days or longer to crisp the pickles. **Yield: 1 quart.**

Note: To double this recipe, you will only need 1½ times the amount of syrup. These pickles sell out before they ever get to the biennual lake flea market.

TIMESAVING BROWN ROUX
IN THE MICROWAVE

²⁄₃ cup vegetable oil
²⁄₃ cup flour

Combine the oil and flour in a microwave-safe bowl or measure and mix
well. Microwave on High for 6 minutes; stir. Microwave for 1 minute;
mixture should be the color of peanut butter. Stir the roux into soups or
gumbos until desired color is reached. You may also add flour to cooked
roux to increase its thickening ability. **Yield: 1¹⁄₃ cups.**

*Note: Just like the authentic type that had to be cooked over the stove, stirring
for up to an hour, this roux is a big timesaver.*

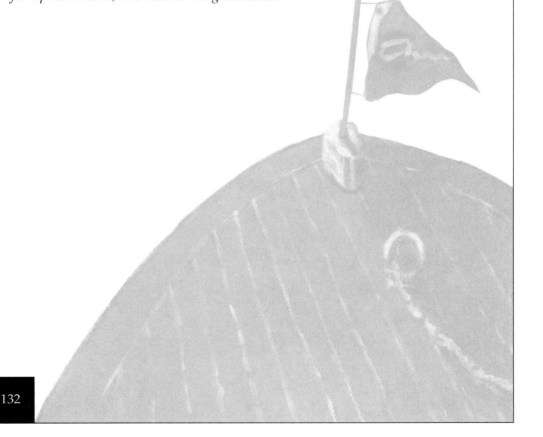

Peanut Jade Marinade

³/₄ cup soy sauce
¹/₂ cup vegetable oil or olive oil
¹/₄ cup white vinegar
2 tablespoons grated fresh gingerroot
¹/₄ to ¹/₃ cup smooth or chunky peanut butter

Combine the soy sauce, oil, vinegar and gingerroot in a bowl and mix well. Add the peanut butter and mix well. Use as a marinade for chicken, salmon or pork, or as a dipping sauce for chicken or pork tenderloin as an appetizer or entrée. The marinade is also good on noodles. **Yield: 1³/₄ cups.**

Note: Cut meat into bite-size pieces for cocktail cruising. This recipe is adapted from a popular Asian technique called satay. It may be enhanced with the addition of minced garlic, grated lemon zest and a few dashes of hot red pepper sauce.

GARLIC SAUCE OR TUM-BIZ-ZAYT

3 garlic cloves
Salt to taste
1/2 cup olive oil

1/4 cup lemon juice
1/2 cup fresh parsley, finely
  chopped (optional)

Combine the garlic and salt on a plate. Mash the garlic. Combine the garlic mixture, olive oil, lemon juice and parsley in a food processor or blender. Process until blended. Use on salads or as a marinade for grilled chicken. **Yield: 3/4 cup.**

NO POTS OR PANS HOLLANDAISE SAUCE

3 egg yolks
1 1/4 tablespoons fresh lemon juice
1/2 cup (1 stick) unsalted butter,
  softened

Salt to taste
Pinch of cayenne pepper, or
  to taste

Whip the egg yolks in a 4-cup glass measure, adding lemon juice while whipping. Cut the butter into 3 equal portions. Add 1/3 of butter to egg yolk mixture. Microwave, uncovered, on High for 30 seconds. Beat until the butter is completely melted. Add the second piece of butter. Microwave for 30 seconds and beat until the butter is completely melted. Repeat the procedure. Season with salt and cayenne pepper. If the sauce curdles, add 1 tablespoon boiling water and whisk vigorously until creamy and thick. **Yield: 1 cup.**

The Best Barbecue Sauce

¼ cup chopped onion
1 garlic clove, minced
¼ cup vegetable oil
1 cup honey
1 cup ketchup
1 cup vinegar
½ cup Worcestershire sauce
1½ teaspoons salt
1 teaspoon pepper
1 tablespoon dry mustard
1 teaspoon oregano
½ teaspoon thyme

Cook the onion and garlic in the oil in a large skillet until tender, stirring constantly. Add the honey, ketchup, vinegar, Worcestershire sauce, salt, pepper, dry mustard, oregano and thyme. Bring to a boil, stirring constantly. Reduce the heat to low. Simmer for 5 minutes, stirring occasionally. Pour into a jar with a tight-fitting lid. Store in the refrigerator. **Yield: 1 quart.**

Note: You may double or triple this recipe. This sauce is considered number one by anyone fortunate enough to have tried it.

FROM FISH TO VEGGIES SAUCE

½ cucumber, peeled
½ cup sour cream
⅓ cup mayonnaise
2 teaspoons grated onion
2 tablespoons tarragon
¼ teaspoon curry powder
Salt and pepper to taste
2 tablespoons chili sauce (optional)

Seed the cucumber and chop finely. Combine the cucumber, sour cream, mayonnaise, onion, tarragon, curry powder, salt, pepper and chili sauce in a bowl and mix well. Chill, covered, until serving time. Serve with fish, chicken or beef, or as a dip for vegetables. **Yield: 20 tablespoons.**

TARTAR SAUCE

1 cup mayonnaise
1/4 cup minced dill pickle
2 tablespoons minced shallots
2 tablespoons drained capers

1/2 teaspoon tarragon
2 tablespoons Dijon mustard
2 tablespoons minced fresh parsley
1 teaspoon fresh lemon juice

Combine the mayonnaise, pickle, shallots, capers, tarragon, Dijon mustard, parsley and lemon juice in a bowl and mix well. Chill, covered, for 30 minutes or up to 1 week before serving. Recipe may be halved. **Yield: 1½ cups.**

BLENDER MAYONNAISE

1 egg
1/2 teaspoon dry mustard
2 tablespoons vinegar

2 tablespoons lemon juice
1/2 teaspoon salt
1 cup vegetable oil

Combine the egg, dry mustard, vinegar, lemon juice and salt in a blender. Process until blended. Add the oil 1/4 cup at a time, processing constantly until blended. Store in a covered container in the refrigerator. **Yield: 1¼ cups.**

FROM BOAT CHURCH
TO WOODEN BOAT REGATTAS

Boat Church was established in 1980 through the efforts of Stuart Witham and the First Clayton Methodist Church. Lake residents and guests can come by land or sea (in their boats) to a floating service on Sundays during the summer months. The preacher's pulpit is on a floating barge and includes a choir from the local church youth group. Boat Church is a much anticipated weekly tradition for many lake residents and visitors—a unique experience.

Lake Rabun is home to more than 100 wooden boats, and the owners proudly display them on the Fourth of July in the annual "Wooden Boat Regatta Parade." Everyone gets into the patriotic spirit with costumes, decorated boats, and boathouses. The parade is led by the Lakemont-Wiley Volunteer Fire Department Fire Boat, which sprays water high into the air. Along the lakeside, docks are filled with flag-waving children and adults—a very patriotic sight.

Rosemary Focaccia

2 tablespoons dry yeast
1 tablespoon sugar
1¹/₂ cups lukewarm water
¹/₂ cup olive oil
2 teaspoons salt
¹/₃ cup chopped fresh rosemary
5 cups unbleached flour
2 tablespoons butter
2 tablespoons brown sugar
2 medium onions, thinly sliced

Dissolve the yeast and sugar in the lukewarm water in a large mixing bowl. Let stand until foamy. Add the olive oil, salt and rosemary. Beat with the paddle blade of an electric mixer until well mixed. Add the flour gradually, beating constantly at low speed until a soft dough forms. Let stand, covered, until doubled in bulk. Punch the dough down. Spread on a greased baking sheet. Melt the butter in a skillet over medium-high heat. Add the brown sugar. Cook until dissolved, stirring constantly. Add the onions. Cook until caramelized, stirring constantly. Arrange on top of the dough. Let stand, covered, for 30 minutes. Bake at 375 degrees for 35 to 40 minutes or until golden brown. **Yield: 10 servings.**

GRANNY'S ROLLS

1 envelope dry yeast
1 teaspoon sugar
1/4 cup lukewarm water
1/3 cup sugar
1/2 cup shortening

1 egg
1 teaspoon salt
1 cup lukewarm water
4 cups flour
1/2 cup (1 stick) butter, melted

Dissolve the yeast and 1 teaspoon sugar in 1/4 cup lukewarm water in a bowl; set aside. Cream 1/3 cup sugar and shortening with a spoon in a 4-quart bowl. Beat in the egg with a spoon. Add the salt, 1 cup lukewarm water and the yeast mixture and stir to mix well; mixture will be lumpy. Add the flour and stir just until moistened; do not overmix. Cover loosely with a clean kitchen towel. Let rise in a warm place for 2 hours or until doubled in bulk. You may rub the top of the dough lightly with shortening to prevent the top of the dough from hardening while rising. Punch the dough down. Divide the dough into 24 portions. Shape each portion into an oval. Dip the top of each roll in the butter. Fold in half, enclosing the butter. Arrange the rolls with sides touching in a baking pan. Brush lightly with the remaining butter. Cover with a clean kitchen towel. Let rise for 2 hours or until doubled in bulk. Bake at 375 degrees for 20 minutes or until golden brown. You may cover the rolls with plastic wrap and chill overnight before the second rising. Remove the plastic wrap. Cover with a clean kitchen towel. Let rise in a warm place for 2 hours before baking. **Yield: 2 dozen rolls.**

Note: Granny said anybody can make these rolls, and people will love them. No extra butter is needed. The rolls are fun to make for friends for a holiday gift.

Sour Cream Salsa Corn Bread

2 cups self-rising cornmeal
1 cup sour cream
3 eggs, lightly beaten

½ cup salsa
¼ cup vegetable oil

Heat a 10-inch ovenproof skillet in a 400-degree oven for 5 minutes.
Combine the cornmeal, sour cream, eggs, salsa and oil in a bowl and mix
well. Pour into the prepared skillet. Bake for 30 minutes or until golden
brown. **Yield: 8 to 10 servings.**

Best Hush Puppies Ever

1 cup self-rising flour
1 cup self-rising cornmeal
2 tablespoons sugar
1 cup beer, milk or buttermilk

1 egg, lightly beaten
1 cup chopped onion
Vegetable oil for deep-frying

Combine the flour, cornmeal and sugar in a medium bowl and mix
well. Add the beer and egg and mix well. Stir in the onion. Drop by
tablespoonfuls into hot oil in a deep skillet. Fry for 1 to 2 minutes or
until light brown. Remove to paper towels to drain. You may sauté
the onions before adding to the batter. **Yield: 8 servings.**

Note: This recipe makes very light hush puppies that are great with fish.

142

CHERRY ALMOND BRAID

8 ounces cream cheese, softened
1/4 cup sugar
1/2 teaspoon almond extract
1/3 cup chopped maraschino cherries
1/4 cup slivered almonds
2 (8-count) packages crescent rolls
1 cup confectioners' sugar
1 to 2 tablespoons milk
1 tablespoon butter, melted

Beat the cream cheese and sugar in a mixing bowl until fluffy. Add the almond extract and mix well. Fold in the maraschino cherries and almonds. Unroll the crescent roll dough. Arrange the rectangles on a baking sheet to form a 12-inch square, pressing the perforations to seal. Spread the cream cheese mixture over the dough within 1 inch of the top and bottom. Bring 2 sides together to enclose the filling and pinch to seal. Score the top of the loaf at $1^1/4$- to $1^1/2$-inch intervals. Bake at 375 degrees for 25 to 30 minutes or until brown. Remove to a wire rack to cool completely. Combine the confectioners' sugar, milk and butter in a bowl and mix well. Pour over the top of the loaf. Garnish with additional maraschino cherries and almonds.
Yield: 8 to 10 servings.

CHOCOLATE CHIP COFFEE RING

1/2 cup (1 stick) butter, softened
1 cup sugar
2 eggs
1 cup sour cream
1 teaspoon vanilla extract
2 cups flour
1 teaspoon baking powder
1 teaspoon baking soda
1/2 teaspoon salt
1 teaspoon cinnamon

1 cup (6 ounces) semisweet
*   chocolate chips*
1/2 cup packed light brown sugar
1/2 cup flour
1 1/2 teaspoons baking cocoa
1/4 cup (1/2 stick) butter, softened
1/2 cup pecans
1/2 cup (3 ounces) semisweet
*   chocolate chips*

Cream 1/2 cup butter and the sugar in a mixing bowl. Beat in the eggs.
Add the sour cream and vanilla and mix well. Combine 2 cups flour, the
baking powder, baking soda, salt and cinnamon in a bowl and mix well.
Add to the creamed mixture and mix well. Fold in 1 cup chocolate chips.
Combine the brown sugar, 1/2 cup flour, baking cocoa, 1/4 cup butter and
pecans in a bowl and mix well. Spray a bundt pan or 9×9-inch baking
pan with nonstick cooking spray. Sprinkle 3 tablespoons of the brown
sugar mixture over the bottom of the prepared pan. Add half the batter.
Add 1/2 cup chocolate chips to the remaining brown sugar mixture and
mix well. Pour over the batter in the pan. Add the remaining batter. Bake
at 350 degrees for 55 to 60 minutes for the bundt pan or 45 to 50 minutes
for the baking pan. Let stand to cool for 20 minutes before removing
from the pan. **Yield: 8 to 10 servings.**

EASY CINNAMON ROLLS

¹/₂ cup (1 stick) butter or margarine, softened
¹/₄ cup packed light brown sugar
1 tablespoon cinnamon
3 cups baking mix
1 cup buttermilk
¹/₃ cup chopped pecans (optional)
1 cup confectioners' sugar
1 tablespoon milk, cream or orange juice

Combine the butter, brown sugar and cinnamon in a bowl and mix well.
Combine the baking mix and buttermilk and mix until a stiff dough
forms, adding additional baking mix if needed. Roll or pat the dough
into a 10×12-inch rectangle on a floured surface. Spread the butter
mixture evenly over the dough. Sprinkle with the pecans. Roll as for a
jelly roll from one long side. Cut into twelve ³/₄-inch slices. Arrange on a
baking sheet, flattening into ¹/₂-inch-thick rounds. Bake at 425 degrees
for 10 to 12 minutes or until light brown. Let stand to cool slightly.
Combine the confectioners' sugar and milk in a bowl and mix until
smooth. Brush over the warm rolls. Serve immediately. **Yield: 12 rolls.**

*Note: To feed a crowd, make a second batch instead of doubling the recipe. Let
the children help you make these. They are easy, messy and good.*

ORANGE BREAD

1 teaspoon cinnamon
¾ cup sugar
½ cup chopped walnuts
1 tablespoon grated orange zest
2 (10-count) cans refrigerated buttermilk biscuits
3 ounces cream cheese, cut into 20 pieces
½ cup (1 stick) butter, melted
1 cup confectioners' sugar
2 tablespoons orange juice

Combine the cinnamon, sugar, walnuts and orange zest in a bowl and mix well. Separate each biscuit into 2 rounds. Place a piece of cream cheese in the middle of each round. Top with a second round. Pinch the edges to seal. Dip in the butter. Coat with the cinnamon mixture. Stand the biscuits with sides touching in a 12-cup bundt pan. Drizzle with the remaining butter. Sprinkle with the remaining cinnamon mixture. Bake at 350 degrees for 45 minutes. Invert immediately onto a serving plate. Combine the confectioners' sugar and orange juice in a bowl and mix well. Drizzle over the warm bread. **Yield: 10 to 12 servings.**

BEST-EVER BLUEBERRY MUFFINS

1/2 cup (1 stick) butter, softened
1 cup sugar
2 eggs
1 teaspoon vanilla extract
2 teaspoons baking powder
1/4 teaspoon salt
2 cups flour
1/2 cup milk
2 1/2 cups blueberries
1 tablespoon sugar
1/4 teaspoon nutmeg

Beat the butter in a medium mixing bowl until creamy. Beat in 1 cup
sugar until fluffy and pale. Beat in the eggs 1 at a time. Add the vanilla,
baking powder and salt and mix well. Fold in half the flour and half
the milk. Fold in the remaining flour and milk. Mash 1/2 cup of the
blueberries with a fork. Fold the mashed and whole blueberries into
the batter. Fill each of 12 greased muffin cups 3/4 full. Sprinkle with
a mixture of 1 tablespoon sugar and nutmeg. Bake at 375 degrees for
25 to 30 minutes. Let stand to cool for 30 minutes before removing
from pan. Serve with honey butter. **Yield: 12 muffins.**

Herta's Favorite Bran Muffins

2 cups 100% bran cereal
2½ cups sifted unbleached flour
2½ teaspoons baking soda
¾ teaspoon salt
½ teaspoon cinnamon
1 cup apple juice
1 cup 100% bran cereal
½ cup canola oil
5 baby carrots
2 eggs
1 cup buttermilk
2 teaspoons butter flavoring
Raisins (optional)

Process 2 cups cereal in a blender until finely ground. Combine the cereal, flour, baking soda, salt and cinnamon in a bowl and mix well. Bring the apple juice to a boil in a saucepan. Remove from the heat. Stir in 1 cup cereal. Fold into the flour mixture. Combine the canola oil, carrots, eggs, buttermilk and butter flavoring in a blender. Process until well blended. Fold into the flour mixture. Fill muffin cups ³/4 full. Bake at 375 degrees for 12 to 15 minutes. You may substitute 1 cup milk mixed with 1 teaspoon lemon juice for the buttermilk. You may store the batter in jars with tight-fitting lids in the refrigerator for 4 weeks. Use as needed. **Yield: 30 muffins.**

SCALLION AND GOAT CHEESE MUFFINS

4 ounces crumbled goat cheese
1 cup milk
1¹/₂ cups flour
1 tablespoon baking powder
¹/₂ teaspoon salt
1¹/₂ teaspoons sugar
¹/₄ cup (¹/₂ stick) butter, melted
1 egg
1 bunch scallions, finely chopped

Combine the cheese and 2 tablespoons of the milk in a bowl and mix until smooth. Sift the flour, baking powder, salt and sugar into a bowl. Combine the butter, egg and remaining milk in a bowl and whisk until well mixed. Add to the flour mixture and mix well. Stir in the scallions. Divide half the batter among 12 muffin cups. Divide the cheese mixture among the muffin cups. Top with the remaining batter. Bake at 400 degrees for 20 minutes or until golden brown. **Yield: 12 muffins.**

Sinful Cheese Biscuits

2 cups self-rising flour
¹/₂ cup (1 stick) unsalted butter, softened
1 cup (4 ounces) shredded extra-sharp Cheddar cheese
1 cup buttermilk
¹/₂ to 1 cup flour

Combine 2 cups self-rising flour and the butter in a bowl and mix with hands until the mixture resembles coarse meal. Stir in the cheese. Add the buttermilk and mix well. Place ¹/₂ to 1 cup flour on a piece of waxed paper. Roll ¹/₄ cup of the dough at a time in the flour, shaking off any excess flour. Shape into biscuits. You may use more dough for larger biscuits. Arrange the biscuits with sides touching on an ungreased baking sheet. Let stand for 30 minutes. Preheat the oven to 500 degrees. Reduce the oven temperature to 475 degrees. Bake the biscuits for 10 to 15 minutes or until brown. **Yield: 16 biscuits.**

Note: You will get many raves for these biscuits. A slice of country ham goes well with them.

Baked Apple Pancake

2 tablespoons fresh lemon juice
1/2 teaspoon cinnamon
1/4 cup sugar
2 Granny Smith apples, peeled and sliced
6 tablespoons butter
4 eggs
1/2 cup milk
3/4 cup flour
1/4 cup packed dark brown sugar
1/4 cup sour cream
2 tablespoons maple syrup

Combine the lemon juice, cinnamon and sugar in a medium bowl and mix well. Add the apples and toss to coat. Melt the butter in a 10-inch ovenproof nonstick skillet. Pour half the melted butter into a medium bowl and reserve. Add the apple mixture to the butter in the skillet. Sauté until the apples are tender and slightly caramelized. Let stand to cool. Add the eggs, milk and flour to the reserved butter and mix until only small lumps remain. Spread the apples evenly in the skillet. Pour the batter carefully over the apples. Bake at 425 degrees for 10 to 15 minutes or until the bottom is brown and the top is set. Invert onto a greased baking sheet. Sprinkle the pancake with the brown sugar. Bake for 5 minutes or until the top is brown and the brown sugar is bubbly. Cut into wedges. Combine the sour cream and maple syrup in a bowl and mix well. Serve with the pancake. **Yield: 4 servings.**

Note: This pancake is a sweet that is not too sweet.

ORANGE FRENCH TOAST

8 eggs, lightly beaten
1/2 cup sugar
1/2 teaspoon nutmeg
1 1/3 cups orange juice
2/3 cup milk
1 teaspoon vanilla extract
12 (1-inch) slices challah
2/3 cup butter, melted
1/2 cup chopped pecans (optional)
Confectioners' sugar

Combine the eggs, sugar, nutmeg, orange juice, milk and vanilla in a bowl and mix well. Arrange the bread in a single layer in shallow dishes. Pour the egg mixture over the bread. Chill, covered, overnight, turning once. Pour the butter evenly over 2 baking sheets. Arrange the bread over the butter. Bake at 400 degrees for 10 minutes. Sprinkle with the pecans. Bake for 10 minutes longer or until brown. You may cook on medium on a griddle until brown on both sides. Sprinkle with pecans. Arrange on baking sheets. Bake at 200 degrees for 10 minutes or longer to finish cooking or to keep warm until serving time. Cover with foil if keeping warm for longer than 15 minutes. Sprinkle with confectioners' sugar. Serve with maple syrup or preserves. **Yield: 6 servings.**

Note: You may substitute French or sourdough bread for the challah. More slices will be required.

From Glen-Ella Springs Inn, Clarksville, Georgia

Roasted Vegetable Strata

1¹/₂ cups chopped yellow or white
    onions
1 cup finely chopped green onions
12 ounces mushrooms, sliced
8 ounces zucchini, cut into
    ¹/₂-inch pieces
3 tomatoes, coarsely chopped
4 red, green or yellow bell
    peppers or combination,
    cut into 1-inch pieces
¹/₂ cup olive oil or vegetable oil

Salt and pepper to taste
12 eggs
3¹/₂ cups milk, half-and-half or
    heavy cream or combination
3 tablespoons Dijon mustard
Hot red pepper sauce to taste
9 cups (1-inch) Italian bread cubes
2¹/₂ cups (10 ounces) shredded
    extra-sharp Cheddar cheese
1 cup grated Parmesan cheese

Place the onions, green onions, mushrooms, zucchini, tomatoes and bell peppers in a baking pan. Drizzle with the olive oil. Sprinkle generously with salt and pepper. Roast at 425 degrees for 20 to 30 minutes or until tender and light brown, stirring every 10 minutes. Let stand to cool; drain. Combine the eggs, milk, Dijon mustard and pepper sauce in a bowl and whisk to mix well. Arrange half the bread in a buttered shallow 4-quart baking dish. Spread half the vegetable mixture over the bread. Sprinkle with half the Cheddar cheese and Parmesan cheese. Layer with the remaining bread, vegetable mixture and cheeses. Pour the egg mixture evenly over the strata, pressing the layers if needed to cover with the egg mixture. Chill, covered, overnight. Let stand at room temperature while oven preheats to 350 degrees. Bake for 1 hour or until puffed and brown and center is set. Let stand for 15 to 30 minutes before serving. **Yield: 8 servings.**

Note: You may use whatever cheese and vegetables you have on hand. This strata is great with kielbasa and fresh fruit.

Eggs Florentine

9 eggs
2 cups low-fat cottage cheese
4 ounces (1 cup) shredded sharp Cheddar cheese
$^1/_2$ cup crumbled feta cheese
$^1/_2$ teaspoon nutmeg
$^1/_2$ teaspoon salt
$^1/_2$ teaspoon white pepper
2 (10-ounce) packages frozen chopped spinach, thawed and drained
1 red bell pepper, thinly sliced

Whisk the eggs in a large bowl. Whisk in the cottage cheese, Cheddar cheese, feta cheese, nutmeg, salt and white pepper. Stir in the spinach. Pour into a 9×13-inch baking dish sprayed with nonstick cooking spray. Arrange the bell pepper on top. Bake at 375 degrees for 45 minutes or until set. Cool slightly on a wire rack before serving. **Yield: 8 servings.**

Note: You may mix the ingredients ahead of time except for the eggs.

Scrambled Eggs with Cheese and Basil

12 eggs
½ teaspoon seasoned salt
2 ounces cream cheese, cut into small cubes
2 tablespoons unsalted butter
4 fresh basil leaves

Combine the eggs, seasoned salt and cream cheese in a blender. Process until well blended. Melt the butter in a nonstick skillet over low heat. Add the egg mixture. Cook until almost set, stirring constantly. Chop the basil quickly and add to the eggs. Cook until the eggs are done, stirring constantly. **Yield: 6 servings.**

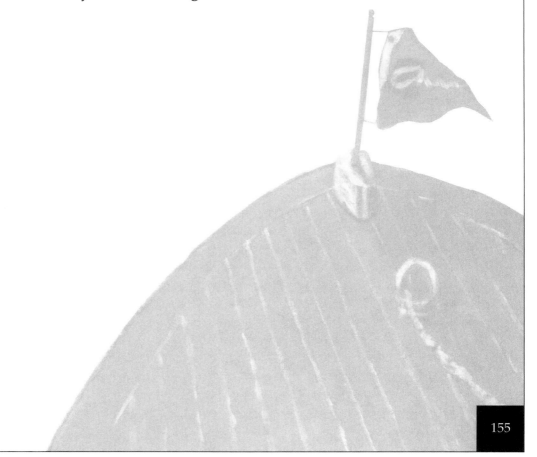

SALSA EGG BAKE

1 (16-ounce) jar mild or medium salsa
1 cup cottage cheese
16 ounces Monterey Jack cheese, cubed
9 eggs
1 cup buttermilk

Spread the salsa over the bottom of a 9×13-inch baking dish. Layer with the cottage cheese and Monterey Jack cheese. Beat the eggs in a mixing bowl. Add the buttermilk and mix well. Pour over the cheese. Bake at 425 degrees for 1 hour. **Yield: 6 to 8 servings.**

Note: You may prepare this dish the night before and chill, covered, overnight. Bake the next day.

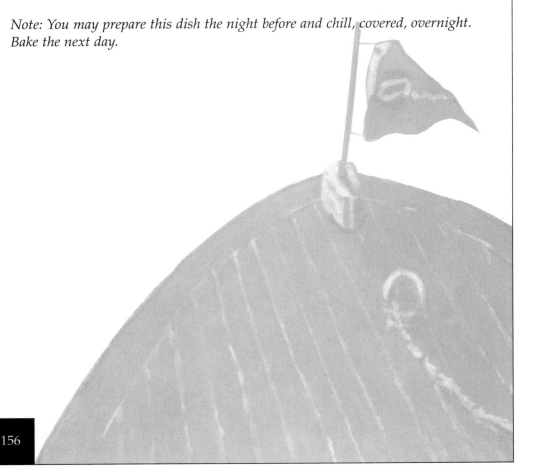

GLEN-ELLA SPRINGS' DELICIOUS EGG CASSEROLE

¼ cup (½ stick) butter
¼ cup flour
½ teaspoon salt
2 cups milk
½ cup (2 ounces) shredded sharp Cheddar cheese
4 eggs, hard-cooked and sliced
1 cup chopped cooked bacon or ham (optional)
1 cup coarse fresh bread crumbs
¼ cup (½ stick) butter, melted

Melt ¼ cup butter in a saucepan over low heat. Blend in the flour and salt. Add the milk all at once. Cook until thickened and bubbly, stirring constantly. Remove from the heat. Add the cheese and stir until melted. Arrange the eggs in the bottom of a buttered shallow baking dish or 4 individual ovenproof dishes. Sprinkle with the bacon. Spread the cheese sauce over the eggs. Combine the bread crumbs with the melted butter and toss to coat. Sprinkle over the sauce. Bake at 400 degrees for 5 minutes or until the bread crumbs are brown and the casserole is heated through. **Yield: 4 servings.**

Note: This recipe may easily be doubled or tripled. Prepare ahead, cover, and chill. Bake just before serving.

From Glen-Ella Springs Inn, Clarksville, Georgia

Sausage and Wild Rice Casserole

2 pounds mild or hot bulk pork sausage
1 package long grain and wild rice with seasonings
¼ cup chopped onion
1 tablespoon soy sauce
2½ cups water
½ cup slivered almonds

Brown the sausage in a skillet, stirring until crumbly; drain. Combine the sausage, rice with seasonings and onion in a bowl and mix well. Chill, covered, for 8 hours or longer. Combine the soy sauce and water in a bowl and mix well. Add to the sausage mixture and mix well. Spoon into a 9×13-inch baking dish. Sprinkle with the almonds. Bake, covered, at 350 degrees for 1 hour. **Yield: 10 servings.**

Note: Serve with scrambled eggs and broiled tomatoes.

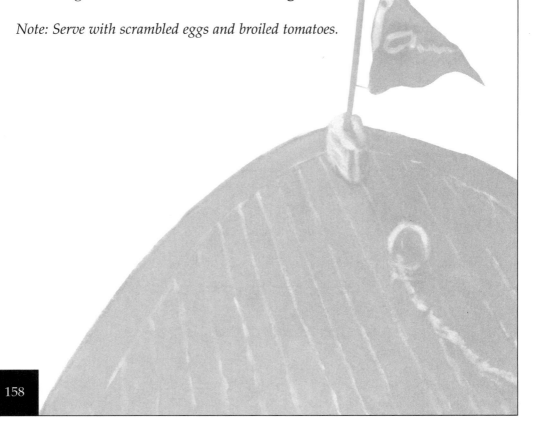

Breakfast Sausage Grits Casserole

1 pound hot bulk pork sausage
2 cups water
1/2 teaspoon salt
1 cup grits
1/8 teaspoon garlic powder
1/4 cup (1/2 stick) butter
1 cup milk
4 eggs, beaten
3 cups (12 ounces) shredded sharp Cheddar cheese

Brown the sausage in a skillet, stirring until crumbly; drain. Bring the water and salt to a boil in a 3-quart saucepan. Add the grits and garlic powder. Cook until thickened, stirring constantly. Add the butter and milk and mix well. Add the eggs, stirring constantly. Reserve 1/2 cup of the cheese. Fold the remaining cheese and sausage into the grits mixture. Spoon into a lightly greased 2-quart baking dish. Bake at 350 degrees for 15 minutes. Sprinkle with the reserved cheese. Bake for 15 minutes longer or until the mixture is puffed and the top is light brown.
Yield: 6 servings.

Note: You may make this the day before and chill, covered, overnight. Bake the next morning. If you double the recipe, don't double the milk. This recipe freezes well.

Low Country Shrimp and Grits

6 slices bacon, chopped
2 tablespoons peanut oil
2 cups sliced mushrooms
1 cup finely sliced scallions
1 pound fresh shrimp, peeled and
    deveined
1 large garlic clove, pressed

4 teaspoons lemon juice
Dash of hot red pepper sauce
2 tablespoons chopped fresh
    parsley
Salt and pepper to taste
Grits

Sauté the bacon in a large skillet just until the edges begin to brown. Remove to a plate. Add the peanut oil to the bacon drippings. Cook until hot. Add the mushrooms and scallions. Sauté for 4 minutes. Add the shrimp. Cook just until the shrimp turn pink, stirring constantly. Stir in the garlic, lemon juice, pepper sauce and parsley. Season with salt and pepper. Divide the shrimp mixture and grits evenly among 6 individual serving plates and serve. **Yield: 6 servings.**

Grits

4 1/2 cups water
1 teaspoon salt
1 cup grits

Butter
1/2 cup shredded Cheddar cheese

Combine the water and salt in a saucepan. Bring to a boil. Add the grits gradually, whisking constantly. Reduce the heat to low. Add butter and the cheese, stirring constantly. Cook over low heat for 30 minutes, stirring frequently.

SAUSAGE PINWHEELS

1 large frozen puff pastry sheet, thawed
2 tablespoons Dijon mustard
1 pound mild or hot bulk pork sausage

Brush the surface of the puff pastry with the Dijon mustard. Spread the sausage evenly over the top, leaving a 1/2-inch border on one long side. Roll as for a jelly roll from the other long side and seal the seam. Place seam side down on a baking sheet, reshaping if needed. Freeze, covered, until 1 hour before serving. Thaw slightly. Cut into 1/4-inch slices. Arrange on a baking sheet. Bake at 375 degrees for 20 minutes or until the sausage is cooked through and the pastry is crisp and brown. Drain on paper towels. Serve warm. You may use 4 puff pastry squares in place of 1 large sheet of puff pastry. Arrange on a floured surface to form a large square or rectangle and seal the seams. Roll lightly with a rolling pin to smooth out the seams. **Yield: 6 servings.**

Note: These pinwheels freeze well and are wonderful to have on hand.

MUESLI

1 cup skim milk
2 cups rolled oats
½ cup packed brown sugar
1 large can crushed pineapple, drained
1 apple, chopped
1 cup green and/or red seedless grapes, cut into halves
¼ cup nuts, chopped
2 cups nonfat plain yogurt

Combine the milk, oats, brown sugar, pineapple, apple, grapes, nuts and yogurt in a bowl and mix well. Chill, covered, overnight. Serve topped with additional yogurt and fresh fruit, such as berries, peaches or bananas, for a tasty and attractive breakfast dish. **Yield: 8 to 10 servings.**

Note: This recipe belongs to Sandy Turbidy who has visited Lake Rabun and served this to health-conscious friends there and at Sea Island.

GLEN-ELLA SPRINGS' GRANOLA

½ cup (1 stick) margarine
1½ cups honey
7 cups rolled oats
1 cup sliced almonds
1 cup roasted sunflower seeds
1 cup chopped pecans
1 teaspoon cinnamon
1 cup raisins
1 cup diced dried apricots

Melt the margarine in a saucepan. Add the honey. Cook over low heat until the mixture is thin, stirring constantly; keep warm. Combine the oats, almonds, sunflower seeds, pecans and cinnamon in a bowl and mix well. Add the honey mixture and mix well. Spread evenly over the bottom of 1 or 2 large roasting pans or jelly roll pans. Bake at 275 degrees for 45 minutes or until brown and crisp, stirring every 10 minutes. Stir in the raisins and apricots. Let stand to cool. Store in sealable plastic bags. Use within 1 week or freeze. **Yield: 3 quarts.**

From Glen-Ella Springs Inn, Clarksville, Georgia

FROM FLEA MARKETS
TO HOME TOURS

Families at Lake Rabun have fun working together each year on a charitable fund-raising event—the Lake Rabun Flea Market or Lake Rabun Home Tour—which are held in alternating years. Profits help fund the Lakemont-Wiley Volunteer Fire Department, several four-year college scholarships for Rabun County High School seniors, and various other charitable needs in Rabun County.

Recently, the town of Lakemont has seen a rejuvenation with the restoration of the original buildings. An art gallery, an outdoor furniture builder, an antique store, and a specialty food store have joined Alley's Grocery in the business district. The activity is reminiscent of the olden days with the excitement of the daily stops of the Tallulah Falls train at the Depot.

Extra-Easy Blueberry Cobbler

2 pints blueberries, rinsed and drained
3/4 cup flour
3/4 cup sugar
1 teaspoon baking powder
1 egg, beaten
6 tablespoons butter, melted
1/4 teaspoon cinnamon
1 tablespoon light brown sugar

Spread the blueberries in the bottom of a 6×10-inch baking dish. Combine the flour, sugar, baking powder and egg in a bowl and mix with a fork until the mixture resembles coarse meal; mixture should have some lumps. Sprinkle the mixture over the blueberries. Drizzle with the butter. Combine the cinnamon and brown sugar and mix well. Sprinkle over the top of the cobbler. Bake at 350 degrees for 35 to 40 minutes. Let stand to cool slightly before serving; the sauce will thicken as the cobbler cools. **Yield: 6 servings.**

Note: You may substitute blackberries for the blueberries. This cobbler is great with vanilla ice cream.

Green Shutters' Basic Easy Cobbler

½ cup (1 stick) butter
4 cups fresh or canned fruit
1 cup (or more) sugar
Nutmeg, cinnamon or other spice to taste
1 cup self-rising flour
1 cup whole milk
1 package Jiffy yellow cake mix

Melt the butter in a 9×13-inch baking pan in a 350-degree oven. Add the fruit, sugar and spice and mix well. Combine the flour and milk in a mixing bowl. Beat until blended. Pour over the fruit and mix with a spoon. Sprinkle with the cake mix. Bake for 40 to 50 minutes. **Yield: 8 servings.**

From Green Shutters Restaurant, Clayton, Georgia

Nilla Banana Pudding

45 Nilla vanilla wafers
1/2 cup sugar
1/3 cup flour
Dash of salt
3 egg yolks
2 cups milk

1/2 teaspoon vanilla extract
5 ripe bananas, sliced
   (about 3 1/2 cups)
3 egg whites, at room temperature
1/4 cup sugar

Reserve 10 vanilla wafers for garnish. Combine 1/2 cup sugar, flour and salt in a double boiler. Add the egg yolks and milk and mix well. Cook over boiling water for 10 to 12 minutes or until thickened, stirring constantly. Remove from the heat. Stir in the vanilla. Spread a small amount of the pudding over the bottom of a 1 1/2-quart baking dish. Layer with 1/3 of the remaining vanilla wafers and 1/3 of the bananas. Spread 1/3 cup of the pudding over the bananas. Alternate layers of Nilla wafers, bananas and pudding until all of the ingredients are used, ending with the pudding. Beat the egg whites in a mixing bowl until soft peaks form. Add 1/4 cup sugar gradually, beating constantly until stiff peaks form; beat until stiff but not dry. Spoon over the pudding, sealing to the edge. Bake at 350 degrees for 15 to 20 minutes or until brown. Let stand to cool slightly or refrigerate before serving. Garnish with the reserved vanilla wafers. **Yield: 8 servings.**

Yummy Bananas Supreme

2 slightly green bananas
Lemon juice
2 tablespoons butter
2 tablespoons sugar
1 teaspoon cinnamon

Slice the bananas and place in a bowl. Coat lightly with lemon juice. Melt the butter in a sauté pan. Stir in the sugar and cinnamon. Add the bananas. Sauté just until warm. Serve immediately over vanilla ice cream. **Yield: 4 servings.**

Note: *This recipe may be easily doubled or tripled.*

BLUEBERRY CRUST DESSERT

18 butter crackers, crushed
¼ cup (½ stick) butter, melted
¼ cup sugar
8 ounces cream cheese, softened
½ cup sugar
2 eggs
1 (21-ounce) can blueberry pie filling
8 ounces whipping cream
1 tablespoon sugar (optional)

Combine the crackers, butter, and ¼ cup sugar in a bowl and mix well. Press onto the bottom of an 8×8-inch baking pan. Cream the cream cheese and ½ cup sugar in a mixing bowl. Add the eggs and beat until smooth. Spread over the cracker mixture. Bake at 350 degrees for 25 to 30 minutes. Let stand to cool slightly. Spread the pie filling evenly over the top. Chill, covered, for 8 to 10 hours. Whip the whipping cream and 1 tablespoon sugar in a mixing bowl until stiff peaks form. Cut the dessert into squares to serve. Top with the whipped cream. **Yield: 6 servings.**

Note: After 38 years, this is still a trusted favorite dessert.

Blueberry Nut Crunch

1 (2-layer) package yellow cake mix
1 (20-ounce) can crushed pineapple
3 cups fresh blueberries
1/4 cup sugar
1/2 cup (1 stick) butter or margarine, melted
1 cup pecans
1/2 cup sugar

Spread half the cake mix over the bottom of a greased 9×13-inch baking dish. Spread the undrained pineapple over the cake mix. Sprinkle the blueberries over the pineapple. Sprinkle with 1/4 cup sugar. Sprinkle with the remaining cake mix. Drizzle with the butter. Sprinkle the pecans and 1/2 cup sugar over the top. Bake at 350 degrees for 25 minutes. Press the cake mix with a spoon to cover with the juices. Bake for 15 to 20 minutes longer. **Yield: 8 servings.**

Note: You may use thawed frozen blueberries instead of fresh blueberries. Drain the thawed blueberries before using.

CHERRY DUMP CAKE DESSERT

1 (21-ounce) can cherry pie filling
1 (21-ounce) can apple pie filling
1 package Jiffy yellow cake mix
½ cup (1 stick) butter or margarine, melted
½ cup chopped pecans

Combine the cherry and apple pie fillings in a greased 9×13-inch baking dish and mix well. Spread evenly in the baking dish. Sprinkle with the cake mix. Drizzle with the butter. Sprinkle with the pecans. Bake at 350 degrees for 1 hour. Turn off the oven. Let the cake stand in the oven for 15 minutes. Serve warm with vanilla ice cream.
Yield: 6 to 8 servings.

Note: This dessert is easy and always draws rave reviews.

CARAMEL TOFFEE BOMBE

3/4 cup gingersnaps, crumbled
2 tablespoons butter, melted
1 pint vanilla ice cream, softened
2 (1.4-ounce) toffee candy bars, crushed
1 (12-ounce) jar caramel sauce, heated

Line a 2-quart dish with heavy-duty plastic wrap. Combine the cookie crumbs and butter in a bowl and mix well. Press onto the bottom of the prepared dish. Combine the ice cream and candy in a bowl and mix well. Spoon into the dish, spreading evenly. Freeze, covered, for 8 hours. Invert onto a serving plate, carefully removing the dish and plastic wrap. Cut into wedges and serve with the caramel sauce. **Yield: 4 to 6 servings.**

Note: You may substitute chocolate or toffee crunch ice cream for the vanilla ice cream.

DEATH BY CHOCOLATE

1 jar chocolate fudge topping
¹/₄ cup Kahlúa
2 (6-ounce) packages vanilla instant pudding mix
3 cups milk
3 cups whipping cream
1 frozen pound cake, thawed and diced
Crumbled toffee candy bars

Combine the fudge topping and liqueur in a bowl and mix well.
Combine the pudding mix, milk and cream in a bowl and mix well.
Layer the cake, fudge topping mixture, pudding mixture and candy
¹/₂ at a time in a trifle bowl. Serve immediately or chill, covered, until
serving time. **Yield: 12 servings.**

Ice Cream Sandwich Chocolate Special

2 (6-count) packages ice cream sandwiches
1 jar chocolate fudge sauce
1 jar butterscotch sauce
12 ounces whipped topping
1 teaspoon vanilla extract
1 (2-ounce) package sliced almonds, toasted

Line the bottom of a 9×13-inch dish with the ice cream sandwiches, cutting the sandwiches as needed to fit. Spread the fudge sauce evenly over the sandwiches. Drizzle with the butterscotch sauce. Combine the whipped topping and vanilla in a bowl and mix well. Spread over the top of the dessert. Sprinkle with the almonds. Freeze, covered, until serving time. Let stand to soften slightly before cutting into squares.
Yield: 10 servings.

INSTANT ECLAIRS

2 (3-ounce) packages vanilla instant pudding mix
3 cups 1% or 2 % milk
9 ounces whipped topping
1 package graham crackers
2 ounces semisweet chocolate, melted
3 tablespoons butter, melted
1 teaspoon vanilla extract
3 tablespoons milk
1 tablespoon light corn syrup
1½ cups confectioners' sugar

Combine the pudding mix and milk in a bowl and mix well. Add the whipped topping and mix well. Line a 9×12-inch dish with graham crackers. Alternate layers of the pudding and graham crackers, ending with the graham crackers. Combine the chocolate and butter in a bowl and mix well. Add the vanilla, milk, corn syrup and confectioners' sugar and mix well. Pour evenly over the graham crackers. Chill, covered, for several hours. Cut into squares to serve. **Yield: 24 servings.**

Note: This dessert keeps well in the refrigerator.

Jackie Kennedy's Crème Brûlée

3 cups heavy cream
1 (1-inch) piece vanilla bean
6 egg yolks
6 tablespoons sugar
1/2 cup packed brown sugar

Heat the cream and vanilla bean in a double boiler. Beat the egg yolks and sugar in a mixing bowl until light and creamy. Remove the vanilla bean from the cream. Add the cream gradually to the egg mixture, stirring constantly. Return the mixture to the double boiler. Cook until the custard coats a spoon, stirring constantly. Pour into an 8-inch glass dish. Chill, covered, until serving time. Sprinkle with the brown sugar. Caramelize the brown sugar using a torch or place the dish in a large pan of crushed ice and broil for 1 to 2 minutes. You may substitute $1/4$ teaspoon vanilla extract for the vanilla bean. Stir in the vanilla just before pouring the mixture into the glass dish. **Yield: 6 servings.**

Note: Jackie Kennedy put this recipe in the Congressional cookbook in 1961.

GRAND MARNIER PINEAPPLE

1 cup sugar
½ cup water
½ cup Grand Marnier
1 tablespoon finely grated orange zest
½ cup lime juice
2 fresh pineapples, cut into chunks
Fresh raspberries (optional)

Combine the sugar and water in a saucepan. Bring to a boil. Boil for
1 minute, stirring constantly. Add the Grand Marnier, orange zest and
lime juice and mix well. Place the pineapple in a serving dish. Pour the
sauce over the pineapple. Chill, covered, for 1 to 2 hours, stirring
occasionally. Sprinkle with raspberries. Serve cold with wooden picks for
an appetizer or in small bowls for dessert. **Yield: 6 servings.**

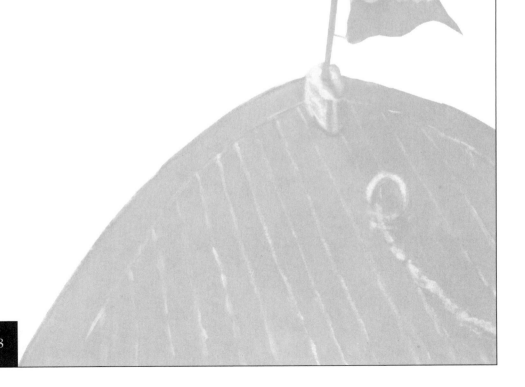

Peaches and Cream Crisp

1 cup sugar
1 egg
1 cup chopped pecans
1 (6-ounce) package vanilla instant pudding mix
1½ cups sour cream
1½ cups milk
2 cups chopped fresh peaches
1 tablespoon lemon juice
8 ounces whipping cream, whipped

Line a baking sheet with foil. Grease the foil. Combine the sugar, egg and pecans in a bowl and mix well. Spread on the prepared baking sheet. Bake at 350 degrees for 18 to 20 minutes. Let stand to cool. Break into small pieces. Combine the pudding mix, sour cream and milk in a bowl and mix well. Combine the peaches and lemon juice in a bowl and mix well. Stir into the pudding mixture. Place a small amount of the pecan mixture in the bottom of each of 8 stemmed sherbet glasses or small bowls. Divide the pudding mixture among the glasses. Sprinkle with the remaining pecan mixture. Chill, covered, for several hours. Top each glass with the whipped cream just before serving. **Yield: 8 servings**

Note: This dish gives new meaning to the expression "peaches and cream."

Peaches aux Vin

6 to 8 peaches
Juice of ¹/₂ lemon
¹/₃ to ¹/₂ cup sugar
1 cup red wine

Peel and slice the peaches. Place in a bowl. Sprinkle with the lemon juice and mix well. Stir in the sugar gently. Chill, covered, for up to 4 hours. Pour the red wine over the peaches 30 minutes before serving. Serve the undrained peaches in wine glasses. **Yield: 4 servings.**

Note: Remove the peels easily from the peaches by first placing them in batches in boiling water in a pan for 20 to 30 seconds. Remove the peaches using a slotted spoon and peel.

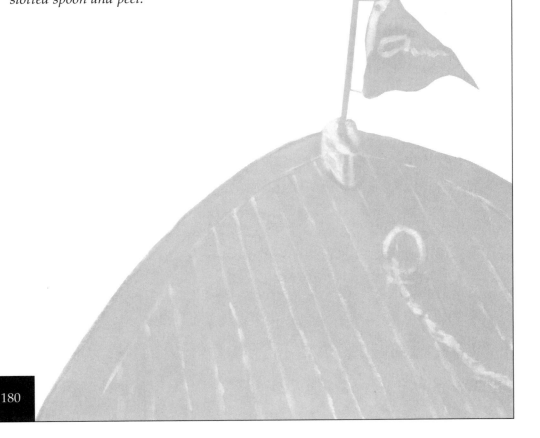

CREAMY FRUIT BEYOND DELICIOUS

2 cups sour cream
1/3 cup packed light brown sugar
Fresh fruit, sliced or chopped
Berries

Combine the sour cream and brown sugar in a bowl and mix well. Chill, covered, for 3 hours or until the brown sugar is dissolved. Drain the fruit and berries if needed. Spoon into a serving dish. Top with the sour cream mixture. Serve with cookies. **Yield: 6 servings.**

Note: You may use reduced-fat sour cream. This is a perfect dessert to satisfy your sweet tooth and your conscience. Try it once and it will become a favorite.

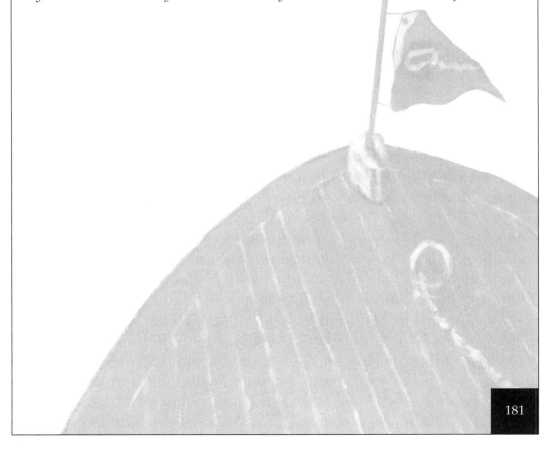

CITRUS POPPY SEED DELIGHT

1⅓ cups orange juice
½ cup vegetable oil
3 eggs
1 (2-layer) package lemon
    cake mix

2 tablespoons poppy seeds
Grated zest of 1 orange
Grated zest of 1 lemon
Citrus Icing

Beat the orange juice, oil and eggs in a mixing bowl. Add the cake mix and beat until moistened. Beat on high for 2 minutes. Fold in the poppy seeds, orange zest and lemon zest. Pour into a bundt pan sprayed with nonstick cooking spray. Bake at 350 degrees for 30 to 35 minutes or until the cake tests done. Invert onto a serving plate. Let stand to cool completely. Spoon the Citrus Icing evenly over the cake. Garnish with additional orange zest and lemon zest. **Yield: 12 servings.**

CITRUS ICING

2 cups (or more) sifted
    confectioners' sugar
2 to 3 tablespoons orange juice

Grated zest of 1 orange
Grated zest of 1 lemon

Combine the confectioners' sugar, orange juice, orange zest and lemon zest in a bowl and mix until thickened, adding additional confectioners' sugar or orange juice if needed for the desired consistency.

Coconut Admonition Cake

1 (2-layer) package white cake mix
2 cups sour cream
1 (1-pound) package confectioners' sugar
9 ounces whipped topping
1 teaspoon vanilla extract
1½ cups shredded coconut

Prepare and bake the cake mix using the package directions for a
9- or 10-inch 2-layer cake. Let stand to cool completely. Cut the layers
horizontally into halves. Combine the sour cream, confectioners'
sugar, whipped topping and vanilla in a bowl and mix well. Reserve
2 tablespoons of the coconut for garnish. Stir the remaining coconut into
the sour cream mixture. Spread between the layers and over the top and
side of the cake. Sprinkle with the reserved coconut. Chill in an airtight
container for 2 days before serving. **Yield: 12 servings.**

Note: This cake is so moist and so good.

STRAWBERRY CAKE

1 (2-layer) package white cake mix
½ cup water
1 (3-ounce) package strawberry gelatin
4 eggs
1 cup canola oil
½ cup frozen strawberries, chopped
Strawberry Frosting

Combine the cake mix, water, gelatin, eggs, canola oil and strawberries in a mixing bowl. Beat at medium speed for 30 seconds. Pour into three 8-inch cake pans or two 9-inch cake pans. Bake at 350 degrees for 25 to 30 minutes or until the layers test done. Spread the Strawberry Frosting between the layers and over the top and side of the cake. This cake keeps well in the refrigerator. **Yield: 12 servings.**

STRAWBERRY FROSTING

¼ cup (½ stick) butter or margarine, melted
½ cup frozen strawberries, chopped and drained
1 (1-pound) package confectioners' sugar

Combine the butter, strawberries and confectioners' sugar in a mixing bowl and mix well.

Fruited Pecan Cake

1 cup shortening or butter, melted
2¼ cups sugar
6 eggs
4 cups self-rising flour
¼ cup orange juice or milk
4 cups pecans, chopped

1 (15-ounce) package golden
   raisins
12 ounces candied pineapple
12 ounces candied cherries
1 tablespoon vanilla extract
Honey or light corn syrup

Combine the shortening and sugar in a mixing bowl and mix well. Beat in the eggs. Add the flour 1 cup at a time, beating constantly. Add the orange juice and mix well. Combine the pecans, golden raisins, pineapple, cherries and a small amount of flour in a bowl and toss to coat. Add to the batter and mix well. Stir in the vanilla. Spoon into a greased 10-inch tube pan. Bake at 275 degrees for 2½ to 3 hours or until the cake tests done, brushing with honey 30 minutes before the cake is done. **Yield: 12 servings.**

Baker's Grease

⅓ cup shortening
⅓ cup vegetable oil

⅓ cup flour

Combine the shortening, oil and flour in a blender or food processor and blend well. You may mix with a fork. Place in a jar or plastic container with a tight-fitting lid. Store in the refrigerator indefinitely. Brush the mixture on pans before adding batter. **Yield: 1 cup.**

Note: Cakes, breads and cookies come out looking like they were done by a pro.

CREAMY BLACKBERRY PIE

3 cups fresh blackberries
1 unbaked (9-inch) deep-dish pie shell
1 cup sugar
1/3 cup flour
1/8 teaspoon salt
2 eggs, beaten
1/2 cup sour cream
1/2 cup sugar
1/2 cup flour
1/4 cup (1/2 stick) butter

Place the berries in the pie shell. Combine 1 cup sugar, 1/3 cup flour and the salt in a bowl and mix well. Add the eggs and sour cream and stir until blended. Spoon the mixture over the blackberries. Combine 1/2 cup sugar and 1/2 cup flour in a bowl and mix well. Cut in the butter until the mixture resembles coarse meal. Sprinkle evenly over the sour cream mixture. Bake at 350 degrees for 50 to 55 minutes or until light brown.
Yield: 6 servings.

Note: When blackberries are not in season, you may use frozen blackberries, which have been thawed and drained.

BUTTERMILK PIE

1 unbaked (9-inch) pie shell
2 cups sugar
3 tablespoons flour
¼ teaspoon nutmeg
½ cup (1 stick) butter, melted
3 eggs, lightly beaten
1 cup buttermilk
3 tablespoons lemon juice
1 teaspoon (rounded) grated lemon zest
1 teaspoon vanilla extract

Bake the pie shell at 350 degrees until partially done. Combine the sugar, flour and nutmeg in a mixing bowl and mix well. Add the butter and beat until creamy. Stir in the eggs, buttermilk, lemon juice, lemon zest and vanilla. Pour into the pie shell. Bake for 1 hour or until a wooden pick inserted in the center comes out clean. **Yield: 6 servings.**

CHOCOLATE ICEBOX PIE

1 (7-ounce) bar chocolate candy with almonds
6 ounces miniature marshmallows
1/2 cup milk
2 cups whipping cream
1 baked (9-inch) piecrust, cooled, or graham cracker pie shell

Combine the candy, marshmallows and milk in a double boiler. Cook until melted, stirring frequently. Let stand to cool. Beat the cream in a mixing bowl until stiff peaks form. Fold half the whipped cream into the chocolate mixture. Spoon into the piecrust. Spread with the remaining whipped cream if desired. **Yield: 6 servings.**

OREO COOKIE COFFEE ICE CREAM PIE

1 (1-pound) package Oreo Chocolate Sandwich Cookies
1/4 cup (1/2 stick) butter, softened
2 quarts vanilla ice cream, softened
3 teaspoons instant coffee granules
1 (5-ounce) can evaporated milk
1/2 cup sugar
1 tablespoon butter
2 ounces semisweet chocolate

Crush the cookies. Combine the cookies and butter in a bowl and mix well. Press onto the bottom of two 9-inch pie plates. Combine the ice cream and coffee granules in a bowl and mix well. Spread over the cookie layer. Freeze until serving time. Combine the evaporated milk, sugar, butter and chocolate in a saucepan. Cook over medium-low heat until the consistency of pudding, stirring constantly. Spread the warm sauce over the pies. Serve immediately. **Yield: 12 servings.**

Ice Cream Pie

1½ quarts vanilla or coffee ice cream or yogurt, softened
1 (9-inch) graham cracker pie shell
5 egg whites
¼ teaspoon cream of tartar
10 tablespoons sugar
Chocolate Sauce

Spoon the ice cream into the pie shell and spread evenly. Beat the egg whites in a mixing bowl until foamy. Add the cream of tartar, beating constantly. Add the sugar, beating constantly until stiff peaks form. Spread over the ice cream. Bake at 475 degrees for 5 minutes or until golden brown. Freeze, covered, for 6 to 8 hours. Drizzle with the warm Chocolate Sauce. Serve immediately. **Yield: 8 to 10 servings.**

Chocolate Sauce

2 ounces unsweetened chocolate
2 tablespoons butter or margarine
1 cup light corn syrup
½ teaspoon vanilla extract

Melt the chocolate in a double boiler. Add the butter and corn syrup. Cook over low heat for 5 minutes, stirring constantly. Stir in the vanilla. You may store the sauce, covered, in the refrigerator.

GRASSHOPPER PIE

7 graham crackers
¼ cup sugar
⅓ cup coarsely chopped walnuts
2 tablespoons baking cocoa
Pinch of salt
¼ cup (½ stick) butter, melted and cooled
2 teaspoons water
2 quarts mint chocolate chip ice cream
Chocolate sauce or hot fudge sauce (optional)

Process the graham crackers in a food processor until crumbly. Add the sugar and walnuts and process until crumbly. Add the baking cocoa, salt, butter and water and process until clumps begin to form. Press over the bottom and up the side of a buttered pie plate. Bake at 350 degrees for 10 minutes. Let stand to cool. Chill for 20 minutes. Let the ice cream soften in the refrigerator for 20 minutes. Spoon the ice cream into the prepared pie shell, spreading evenly. Freeze, covered, until firm. Drizzle with chocolate sauce. Serve immediately. **Yield: 8 to 10 servings.**

Note: Children submitted this recipe for children of all ages.

Key Lime Pie

1¼ cups graham cracker crumbs
½ cup (1 stick) butter, melted
½ cup sugar
½ to 1 cup chopped pecans, toasted
6 egg yolks
¾ cup sweetened condensed milk
¾ cup Key lime juice
6 egg whites
3 tablespoons sugar

Combine the graham cracker crumbs, butter, ¹/₂ cup sugar and pecans in a bowl and mix well. Press over the bottom and up the side of a pie plate. Combine the egg yolks and sweetened condensed milk in a bowl and mix well. Stir in the Key lime juice. Pour into the prepared pie plate. Beat the egg whites in a mixing bowl until soft peaks form. Add 3 tablespoons sugar gradually, beating constantly until stiff peaks form. Spread over the pie. Bake at 350 degrees for 15 minutes. Chill until serving time. **Yield: 6 servings.**

Heavenly Hash Pie

1 (14-ounce) can sweetened condensed milk
¼ cup lemon juice
1 (20-ounce) can crushed pineapple, drained
9 to 12 ounces whipped topping
1 cup pecans, chopped
1 cup flaked coconut
2 graham cracker pie shells

Combine the sweetened condensed milk, lemon juice, pineapple, whipped topping, pecans and coconut in a bowl and mix well. Spoon equal portions of the mixture into each of the pie shells. Garnish with pecan halves. Freeze, covered, until serving time. **Yield: 12 servings.**

GRITS RUM PIE

³/₄ cup water
¹/₈ teaspoon salt
¹/₄ cup quick-cooking grits
¹/₂ cup (1 stick) butter
2 eggs, lightly beaten
³/₄ cup sugar
2 tablespoons flour
¹/₄ cup buttermilk
1 tablespoon rum
1 teaspoon vanilla extract
1 baked (9-inch) pie shell

Combine the water and salt in a saucepan. Bring to a boil. Add the grits. Cook for 4 minutes, stirring constantly. Add the butter. Cook for 1 minute, stirring constantly. Combine the eggs, sugar, flour, buttermilk, rum and vanilla in a bowl and mix well. Add to the grits mixture and mix well. Spoon into the pie shell. Bake at 325 degrees for 35 to 40 minutes or until set. Serve hot or cold. **Yield: 6 servings.**

Note: You may serve the pie with whipped cream and berries.

Apricot Jam Bars

1 cup sugar
2 cups flour
1/2 teaspoon baking soda
1/2 teaspoon salt
3/4 cup (1 1/2 sticks) butter or margarine
1 cup chopped nuts
8 ounces shredded coconut
1 (16-ounce) jar apricot jam

Combine the sugar, flour, baking soda and salt in a bowl and mix well. Cut in the butter with a pastry blender until crumbly. Add the nuts and coconut and mix well. Press 3/4 of the mixture onto the bottom of a greased 9×13-inch baking pan, reserving the remaining mixture. Spread the apricot jam evenly over the top. Sprinkle with the reserved mixture. Bake at 350 degrees for 30 minutes. Cut into bars to serve. **Yield: 12 bars.**

Lemon, Lime and Blueberry Squares

1/2 cup flour
3/4 cup yellow cornmeal
6 tablespoons confectioners' sugar
1/2 teaspoon salt
1/2 cup (1 stick) chilled unsalted
    butter, cut into pieces
3 eggs
1/2 cup sugar

1 1/2 tablespoons flour
1/2 teaspoon lemon zest
1/2 teaspoon lime zest
1 tablespoon fresh lemon juice
1 tablespoon fresh lime juice
2 tablespoons whole milk
2 cups fresh blueberries
3 tablespoons apricot jam, heated

Line a buttered 8×8-inch glass baking dish with two 16×16-inch pieces
of foil, overlapping in opposite directions to leave an overhang on all
4 sides. Combine 1/2 cup flour, cornmeal, confectioners' sugar, salt and
butter in a food processor. Process until the mixture resembles coarse
meal. Press over the bottom and 1 inch up the sides of the prepared dish.
Bake at 375 degrees on the middle oven rack for 20 minutes or until
brown. Combine the eggs, sugar, 1 1/2 tablespoons flour, lemon zest, lime
zest, lemon juice, lime juice and milk in a bowl and whisk until well
mixed. Pour the filling into the crust. Bake for 17 minutes or until set.
Combine the blueberries and apricot jam in a bowl and mix well. Spoon
carefully over the filling. Bake for 2 minutes longer. Cool on a wire rack.
Chill, covered, for 8 hours. Lift out of the dish using the foil overhang.
Cut into squares. Garnish servings with sweetened whipped cream and
lemon slices. **Yield: 9 squares.**

GEORGIA'S EVIL

½ cup (1 stick) butter or margarine, melted
1½ cups graham cracker crumbs
2 cups (12 ounces) mixed chocolate, peanut butter and
*   butterscotch chips*
1¼ cups flaked coconut
1 cup chopped nuts
1 (14-ounce) can sweetened condensed milk

Combine the butter and graham cracker crumbs in a bowl and mix well.
Press onto the bottom of a 9×13-inch baking pan using a fork. Layer with
the mixed chips, coconut and nuts. Pour the sweetened condensed milk
evenly over the layers. Bake at 350 degrees for 20 to 25 minutes or until
light brown. Cool completely or chill, covered, in the refrigerator. You
may store, covered, at room temperature. If using a glass baking dish,
reduce the oven temperature to 325 degrees. **Yield: 2 to 3 dozen bars.**

A Little Bit of Everything Cookies

1 (5-pound) container refrigerated chocolate chip
    cookie dough, softened
1½ cups rolled oats
1 cup chocolate chunks
1 cup (6 ounces) butterscotch chips
1 (8-ounce) package dates, chopped
1 cup (6 ounces) peanut butter chips, or
    12 ounces (2 cups) miniature "M&M's" Chocolate Candies
1 cup chopped walnuts

Combine the cookie dough, oats, chocolate chunks, butterscotch chips, dates, peanut butter chips and walnuts in a large bowl and mix well. Shape the dough into twelve to fifteen 1×12-inch logs. Wrap each log in foil and freeze. To bake, cut into ½-inch slices. Arrange on baking sheets. Bake at 375 degrees for 10 to 15 minutes or until brown.
Yield: 200 cookies.

Note: You may add raisins, dried cranberries or dried cherries to the mixture.

BROWNIE BRICKLE BARS

½ cup (1 stick) butter
2 ounces unsweetened chocolate, chopped
1 cup sugar
2 eggs
1 teaspoon vanilla extract
¾ cup flour
¾ cup almond brickle pieces
½ cup miniature semisweet chocolate chips

Melt the butter and unsweetened chocolate in a medium saucepan over low heat. Remove from the heat. Stir in the sugar, eggs and vanilla. Beat lightly with a wooden spoon until well mixed. Stir in the flour. Spoon into a greased 8×8-inch baking pan. Combine the almond brickle and chocolate chips in a bowl and mix well. Reserve ¼ cup of the mixture. Sprinkle the remaining mixture over the brownies. Bake at 350 degrees for 30 minutes. Sprinkle with the reserved mixture. Let stand to cool. Cut into squares. **Yield: 9 squares.**

CHATTANOOGA CHOO-CHOOS

2 cups flour
1 cup packed light brown sugar
1/2 cup (1 stick) butter, softened
1 cup chopped pecans
1 cup (2 sticks) butter
3/4 cup packed brown sugar
12 ounces (2 cups) semisweet chocolate chips

Combine the flour, 1 cup brown sugar and 1/2 cup butter in a bowl and mix well. Press onto the bottom of a 9×13-inch baking pan. Sprinkle evenly with the pecans. Melt 1 cup butter and 3/4 cup brown sugar in a saucepan. Bring to a boil. Boil for 1 minute, stirring constantly. Pour evenly over the pecans. Bake at 350 degrees for 20 to 25 minutes or until the surface is bubbly. Sprinkle with the chocolate chips. Let stand to cool for 5 hours. Cut into squares. **Yield: 24 squares.**

Butter Chews

³/₄ cup (1¹/₂ sticks) butter, softened
3 tablespoons sugar
1¹/₂ cups flour
3 egg yolks, beaten
1 cup plus 2 tablespoons packed light brown sugar
1 cup plus 2 tablespoons packed dark brown sugar
1 cup chopped nuts
³/₄ cup shredded coconut
3 egg whites, stiffly beaten
Confectioners' sugar

Cream the butter and sugar in a mixing bowl. Blend in the flour. Pour evenly into a greased 8×8-inch baking pan. Bake at 350 degrees for 15 minutes or until light brown. Remove from the oven. Reduce the oven temperature to 325 degrees. Combine the egg yolks and brown sugar in a bowl and mix well. Add the nuts and coconut and mix well. Fold in the egg whites. Spread evenly over the baked layer. Bake for 30 minutes; cool. Cut into bars. Dust with confectioners' sugar. **Yield: 12 bars.**

Irresistible Cookies

1 cup (2 sticks) butter, softened
1 cup sugar
1 cup packed light brown sugar
1 cup vegetable oil
1 egg
Pinch of salt
1 teaspoon baking soda
1 teaspoon vanilla extract
1 cup sweetened cornflakes, crushed
^{1}/$_2$ cup shredded coconut
^{1}/$_2$ cup chopped pecans
3^1/$_2$ cups sifted flour
1 cup rolled oats

Cream the butter, sugar and brown sugar in a mixing bowl. Add the oil and egg and mix well. Add the salt, baking soda, vanilla, sweetened cornflakes, coconut, pecans, flour and oats and mix well. Drop by rounded teaspoonfuls 2 inches apart onto nonstick baking sheets. Bake at 325 degrees for 12 minutes; do not overbake. **Yield: 8 dozen cookies.**

SOFT GINGERSNAP COOKIES

3/4 cup shortening
1 cup sugar
1/4 cup molasses
1 egg
2 teaspoons baking soda
2 cups flour

1/2 teaspoon ground cloves
1/2 teaspoon ginger
1 teaspoon cinnamon
1/2 teaspoon salt
Sugar

Melt the shortening in a saucepan. Let stand to cool. Remove to a
mixing bowl. Add 1 cup sugar, molasses and egg and mix well. Add
the baking soda, flour, cloves, ginger, cinnamon and salt and mix well.
Chill, covered, in the refrigerator. Shape into 1-inch balls. Roll in sugar.
Arrange 2 inches apart on a nonstick baking sheet. Bake at 350 degrees
for 8 minutes. **Yield: 3 dozen cookies.**

CHEESE FUDGE

1 cup chopped pecans
2 (1-pound) packages
    confectioners' sugar
1/2 cup baking cocoa

8 ounces Velveeta cheese
1 cup (2 sticks) butter
1/2 teaspoon vanilla extract

Spread the pecans on a baking sheet. Bake at 300 degrees for 15 to
20 minutes or until toasted; do not burn. Combine the confectioners'
sugar and baking cocoa in a bowl and mix well. Melt the cheese and
butter in a double boiler or heavy saucepan over low heat. Add to the
confectioners' sugar mixture and mix well. Add the vanilla and toasted
pecans and mix well. Pour into a 9×13-inch pan. Cool completely. Cut
into 1 1/2-inch squares. Store in an airtight container. **Yield: 90 squares.**

AMBER PEANUT BRITTLE

1 cup sugar
½ cup light corn syrup
½ cup water
1 cup raw peanuts

1 tablespoon butter
1 teaspoon vanilla extract
2 teaspoons baking soda

Combine the sugar, corn syrup and water in a saucepan. Bring to a boil. Boil to 235 degrees on a candy thermometer, spun thread stage, stirring constantly. Add the peanuts. Cook until the mixture turns amber, stirring constantly. Add the butter, vanilla and baking soda quickly and mix well. Pour quickly onto a buttered large baking sheet; do not spread. Cool completely. Break into pieces. Store in an airtight container. **Yield: variable.**

Note: Have everything measured before beginning. Once the mixture turns amber, everything moves quickly. Do not refrigerate the peanut brittle to speed the cooling process; humidity will make it sticky.

PUPPY CHOW

12 ounces (2 cups) chocolate chips
1 cup creamy peanut butter
1 package rice Chex cereal

1 (1-pound) package confectioners' sugar

Melt the chocolate chips and peanut butter in a saucepan. Place the cereal in a large bowl. Pour the chocolate mixture over the cereal and mix with hands; mixture may be hot. Pour into a clean paper bag. Add the confectioners' sugar and shake to coat. **Yield: 1 large bowlful.**

RESTAURANT RECIPE CONTRIBUTORS

Buck Creek Tavern

Chops/Lobster Bar

Glen-Ella Springs Inn

Green Shutters

Lakemont Provisions

Longhorn Steakhouse

McKinnon's Louisiane Restaurant

Ted's Montana Grill

CONTRIBUTORS

Dr. Sharada Alducin

Gayle Alston

Lynda Anderson

Barrie Aycock

Ed Barber

Lu Barber

Dixie B. Barton

Karen Bellaire

Fran Bondurant

Dawn Boucher

Caroline B. Bowen

Hayden Bowen

Mary Martin Bowen

Evie Bronikowski

Julie Johnson Brooks

Trace Brooks

Sharon Brown

Winnie Brown

Olivia Bruce

Ingrid Brunt

Penny Burkitt

Carol Lee Cathey

Judy Cathey

Lael Seydel Ceravolo

GeeGee Clarke

Melissa Clinkscales

Nita Cofer

Jane Leigh Collier

Bill Collins

Jan Collins

Bonnie Copeland

Susan Cormany

Kathy Cotney

Jeanne Cowan

Marion Croxton

Gail Davenport

Terri Davidson

Mary Deadwyler

Donna K. Deas

Elaine Dickens

Diane Douglas

Elizabeth Duncan

Hadley Hulsey Duncan

Lawson Duncan

Sanford Dunklin

Eryn Dunwody

Helen Dunwody

Janet Dunwody

Dan Dunwody, Jr.

Jill Dyas

Louisa Edmondson

Mary Evans

Mary Meade Evans

Vickie and Leon Farmer

Joyce Fendig

Allison Smith Freeland

Christina Freeman

Judy Freeman

Martha Gaddis

Paula Grayson

Linda Weather Green

Mary V. Grigsby

Shirley Halter

Sue Halter

Lisa Pruitt Hamby

Clara Guy Harrington

Frances Troutman Harris

Dianne Harrison

Kitty McNeely Hartley

Jane Heeney

Elaine Herndon

Phyllis Heyburn

Kay Trogdon Hightower

Lisa Hinson

Wanda S. Hopkins

Harriett Martin Hulsey

Cissy Hutchinson

Gayle Ide

Mrs. R. F. Ingram

Diane Isakson

Mac Jackson

Mary Jackson

Miriam Jackson

Prissy Jenkins

L. Comer Jennings, Jr.

George Johnson

Heather Leigh Johnson

Judy G. Johnson

Kathleen Johnson

Linda J. Johnson

Pilar L. Johnson

Russell Johnson

Bette Jones

Brenda Jones

Luann Jones

Jeni Knight

Jo Ann Lampe

Marilyn Langston

Jean LaRocca

Betty Layng

Felicia Lease

Bill Lee

Peggy Lientz

Beverly Harris Logan

Lisa Longino

Roses Longino

Sherry Lundeen

Cathy Macintyre

Anna Marett

Libby Mathews

Tricia Maypole

Dot McClure

Sue McCoy

Dee McElroy

Billy McKinnon

Marilyn McNeely

Bob McOsker

Marsha McOsker

Helen McSwain

Darcie Johnson Miller

Nate Miller

Libby Mims

Ethel Mitchell

Mary Pat Monfort

Tracey Moody

Donna L. Moore

Betsy Bairstow Morse

Dan Morse

Mary Newkirk

Cathy M. Nix

Frances Chiles Noble

Betty Nunnally

Sandy O'Brien

Bobby Parker

Jennifer Haugen Parker

Anne Pledger

Mary George Poss

Marlee J. Price

Lisa Prickett

Mebane Pruitt

Nancy Pruitt

Paige Pruitt

Carol Raeber

Ruth Read

Beth Reagan

Pat Reeve

Susan Rich

Trudy Richards

Beth Richardson

Penny Robinson

Barbara Persons Roper

Lillian Rowan

Debbie Rust

Dwight Scott

Mary Shannon Scott

Laura Seydel

Rosina Seydel

Scott O. Seydel, Jr.

Susan Sharpe-Dickens

Michele Sharpton

Mimi Shaw

Jean Sheldon

Eleanor Sheriff

B. J. Smith

Kathy Steinbruegge

Tom W. Steinichen

Carol C. Stelling

Margie Stockton

Louellen Stormont

Jennifer W. Stribling

Alison Stromquist

Myra Stromquist

Winanne Sutherland

Julie Taylor

Leslie Thomas

Janet Torrance

Craig Towns

Forrest Towns

Havilyn Hulsey Towns

Julianna Towns

Marimartin Towns

Marihope S. Troutman

Miriam Troutman

Nan Troutman

Velda Turner

Madge Vaughan

Bob and Belle Voyles

Doris L. Warren

Gail M. Watson

Ann Webb

Fran Wechtel

Gertrude Wechtel

Della Weller

Frank Weller

Laura West

Joan Whitney

Peggy Wiggins-Rowan

Susan Williams

Virginia Williams

"Bitty" Wisenbaker

Bunky Witham

Kate S. Worley

Beverly Wright

INDEX

Accompaniments
Garlic Pickles, 131
Gremolata, 78, 84
Hot Pepper and Orange
  Preserves, 130
Triple-Fruit Salsa, 129

Appetizers. *See also* Dips;
  Sandwiches; Spreads
Bacon Cheese Squares, 15
Cream Cheese Roll-Ups, 15
Lake Rabun Salmon
  Bites, 17
Mushroom Squares, 16
Olive Caper Crostini, 16
Pears on Pumpernickel, 17
Poppy Cheese Sticks, 20
Puppy Chow, 203
Scallops in Scotch and
  Cream, 14
Tomato Basil
  Bruschetta, 18

Apples
Ancient Sweet-and-Sour
  Red Cabbage, 109
Baked Apple Pancake, 151
Cherry Dump Cake
  Dessert, 172
Cornucopia Salad, 49
Harvest Brie, 21
Muesli, 162
Mixed Greens with Pears
  and Gorgonzola, 51

Apricots
Apricot Jam Bars, 194
Glen-Ella Springs'
  Granola, 163
Hot Baked Fruit, 128
Lemon, Lime and
  Blueberry Squares, 195

Pork Tenderloin with
  Apricot Sauce, 70

Artichokes
Chicken and Artichoke
  Pizzas, 91
Easy Vegetarian Pasta
  Sauce, 80
Lemon Artichoke
  Hearts, 106
Sausalito Crab
  Dip, 27
Stuffed Tomatoes, 119

Avocados
Cornucopia Salad, 49
Layered Cobb Salad, 48
Roasted Corn
  Guacamole, 26

Bacon
Authentic German Potato
  Salad, 57
Bacon Cheese Squares, 15
BLT Dip, 24
Fried Green Tomato
  Sandwiches, 18
Glen-Ella Springs'
  Delicious Egg
  Casserole, 157
Go with Anything
  Beans, 107
Hot Macaroni Salad, 60
Layered Cobb Salad, 48
Low Country Shrimp and
  Grits, 160
Mushroom Squares, 16
Summer Squash with a
  Twist, 117
Wedge Salad with Bacon,
  Tomato and Chive
  Dressing, 52

Bananas
Nilla Banana Pudding, 168
Yummy Bananas
  Supreme, 169

Beans
Black Bean and Rice
  Salad, 53
Cha Cha Cha Black Bean
  Dip, 24
Championship Chili, 40
Chicken Salsa with Cheese
  Grits Soufflé, 90
Delicious Pumpkin, Black
  Bean and Turkey
  Soup, 34
Easy Vegetarian Pasta
  Sauce, 80
Fireside White Chili, 39
Go with Anything
  Beans, 107
Green Bean Salad, 54
Layered Southwestern
  Salad, 55
Roasted Vegetables, 123
Shrimp and Green Bean
  Salad, 45
Vegetable Casserole, 122

Beef. *See also* Ground Beef;
  Veal
Baked Beef Dip, 25
Beef Tenderloin à la
  Lake, 64
Hot Reuben Dip, 25
Marinated Chuck Roast, 65
Marinated Flank Steak, 67
Old-Fashioned Brunswick
  Stew, 36
Pepper-Seared New York
  Strip, 66
Texas Cool Dip, 26

Beverages
Mango Texas
Margaritas, 31
Mint Tea, 31
Not the Same Old
Homemade Bloody
Mary, 30

Bison
Bison Meat Loaf, 74

Blueberries
Best-Ever Blueberry
Muffins, 147
Blueberry Crust
Dessert, 170
Blueberry Nut Crunch, 171
Extra-Easy Blueberry
Cobbler, 166
Lemon, Lime and
Blueberry Squares, 195

Breads. *See also* Muffins
Baked Apple Pancake, 151
Baker's Grease, 185
Best Hush Puppies
Ever, 142
Cherry Almond Braid, 143
Chocolate Chip Coffee
Ring, 144
Easy Cinnamon Rolls, 145
Granny's Rolls, 141
Orange Bread, 146
Orange French Toast, 152
Rosemary Focaccia, 140
Sinful Cheese Biscuits, 150
Sour Cream Salsa Corn
Bread, 142

Breakfast. *See also* Egg
Dishes
Baked Apple Pancake, 151
Best-Ever Blueberry
Muffins, 147
Breakfast Sausage Grits
Casserole, 159

Cherry Almond Braid, 143
Chocolate Chip Coffee
Ring, 144
Easy Cinnamon
Rolls, 145
Glen-Ella Springs'
Granola, 163
Herta's Favorite Bran
Muffins, 148
Low Country Shrimp and
Grits, 160
Muesli, 162
Orange Bread, 146
Orange French Toast, 152
Sausage and Wild Rice
Casserole, 158
Sausage Pinwheels, 161
Scallion and Goat Cheese
Muffins, 149
Sinful Cheese Biscuits, 150

Broccoli
Broccoli Tomato
Casserole, 108
Tortellini Salad, 58

Cabbage
Ancient Sweet-and-Sour
Red Cabbage, 109
Fish Tacos "A Texas
Thing," 97
Oriental Coleslaw, 54

Cakes
Baker's Grease, 185
Citrus Poppy Seed
Delight, 182
Coconut Admonition
Cake, 183
Fruited Pecan
Cake, 185
Strawberry Cake, 184

Candy
Amber Peanut Brittle, 203
Cheese Fudge, 202

Capers
Chicken Marbella, 86
Easy Vegetarian Pasta
Sauce, 80
Fifteen-Minute Grilled
Salmon with Angel
Hair, 95
Lake Rabun Salmon
Bites, 17
Olive Caper Crostini, 16
Tartar Sauce, 137
Tender Chicken Osker, 88
Veal Scaloppine with
Mushrooms and
Capers, 77

Cherries
Cherry Almond Braid, 143
Cherry Dump Cake
Dessert, 172
Hot Baked Fruit, 128

Chicken
Asian Grilled Chicken
Salad, 46
Chicken and Artichoke
Pizzas, 91
Chicken and Sausage
Gumbo, 35
Chicken Marbella, 86
Chicken Piccata, 85
Chicken Salsa with Cheese
Grits Soufflé, 90
Cornucopia Salad, 49
Fireside White Chili, 39
Grandma's Chicken
Noodle Soup, 38
Grilled Lemon Pepper
Chicken with
Gremolata, 84
Layered Cobb Salad, 48
Marinated Honey Lemon
Chicken, 87
Old-Fashioned Brunswick
Stew, 36
Ro-Tel Chicken Pasta, 89

Tarragon Chicken
  Salad, 47
Tender Chicken Osker, 88

Chocolate
  A Little Bit of Everything
    Cookies, 197
  Brownie Brickle Bars, 198
  Chattanooga Choo-
    Choos, 199
  Cheese Fudge, 202
  Chocolate Chip Coffee
    Ring, 144
  Chocolate Icebox Pie, 188
  Chocolate Sauce, 189
  Death by Chocolate, 174
  Georgia's Evil, 196
  Grasshopper Pie, 190
  Ice Cream Pie, 189
  Ice Cream Sandwich
    Chocolate Special, 175
  Instant Eclairs, 176
  Oreo Cookie Coffee Ice
    Cream Pie, 188
  Puppy Chow, 203

Coconut
  Apricot Jam Bars, 194
  Butter Chews, 200
  Coconut Admonition
    Cake, 183
  Georgia's Evil, 196
  Heavenly Hash Pie, 192
  Irresistible Cookies, 201

Cookies
  A Little Bit of Everything
    Cookies, 197
  Apricot Jam Bars, 194
  Baker's Grease, 185
  Brownie Brickle Bars, 198
  Butter Chews, 200
  Chattanooga Choo-
    Choos, 199
  Georgia's Evil, 196
  Irresistible Cookies, 201

Lemon, Lime and
  Blueberry Squares, 195
Soft Gingersnap
  Cookies, 202

Corn
  Cha Cha Cha Black Bean
    Dip, 24
  Chicken Salsa with Cheese
    Grits Soufflé, 90
  Creamed Corn in the
    Microwave, 110
  Lakemont Provisions'
    Shrimp and Corn
    Salad, 44
  Layered Southwestern
    Salad, 55
  Old-Fashioned Brunswick
    Stew, 36
  Rainy Day Corn
    Chowder, 41
  Roasted Corn
    Guacamole, 26
  Vegetable Casserole, 122

Crab Meat
  Pawleys Island Crab
    Cakes, 98
  Sausalito Crab Dip, 27
  Seafood Pizza, 23
  The Ultimate Crab Dip, 27

Cucumbers
  From Fish to Veggies
    Sauce, 136
  Picnic Cucumber Dill
    Soup, 42
  Turkey Mozzarella Rabun
    Picnic Sandwiches, 19

Desserts. *See also* Cakes;
    Candy; Cookies; Pies
  Blueberry Crust
    Dessert, 170
  Blueberry Nut Crunch, 171
  Caramel Toffee Bombe, 173

Cherry Dump Cake
  Dessert, 172
Creamy Fruit Beyond
  Delicious, 181
Death by Chocolate, 174
Extra-Easy Blueberry
  Cobbler, 166
Grand Marnier
  Pineapple, 178
Green Shutters' Basic Easy
  Cobbler, 167
Ice Cream Sandwich
  Chocolate Special, 175
Instant Eclairs, 176
Jackie Kennedy's Crème
  Brûlée, 177
Nilla Banana Pudding, 168
Peaches and Cream
  Crisp, 179
Peaches aux Vin, 180
Yummy Bananas
  Supreme, 169

Dips. *See also* Salsas
  Baked Beef Dip, 25
  BLT Dip, 24
  Cha Cha Cha Black Bean
    Dip, 24
  Hot Reuben Dip, 25
  Roasted Corn
    Guacamole, 26
  Sausalito Crab Dip, 27
  Spicy Spinach Dip, 28
  Sun-Dried Tomato
    Dip, 29
  Texas Cool Dip, 26
  The Ultimate Crab Dip, 27

Egg Dishes
  Eggs Florentine, 154
  Glen-Ella Springs'
    Delicious Egg
    Casserole, 157
  Roasted Vegetable
    Strata, 153
  Salsa Egg Bake, 156

Scrambled Eggs with
Cheese and Basil, 155

Fish. *See also* Salmon; Tilapia
Ginger-Crusted Grouper
with Orange Jalapeño
Sauce, 94

Frostings/Icings
Citrus Icing, 182
Strawberry Frosting, 184

Fruit. *See also* Apples;
Apricots; Avocados;
Bananas; Blueberries;
Cherries; Coconut;
Lemon; Lime; Oranges;
Peaches; Pears;
Pineapple; Raspberries;
Strawberries
Creamy Blackberry Pie, 186
Creamy Fruit Beyond
Delicious, 181
Fruited Pecan Cake, 185
Green Shutters' Basic Easy
Cobbler, 167

Game Birds
Smothered Quail or
Dove, 93

Grits
Breakfast Sausage Grits
Casserole, 159
Cheese Grits, 90
Grits, 160
Grits Rum Pie, 193

Ground Beef
Championship Chili, 40
Wonderful Meat Loaf, 68

Ham
Glen-Ella Springs' Delicious
Egg Casserole, 157
Holiday Ham Towers, 72

Lamb
Pepper-Crusted Leg of
Lamb, 76
Rack of Lamb, 75

Lemon
Buttermilk Pie, 187
Chicken Piccata, 85
Citrus Icing, 182
Citrus Poppy Seed
Delight, 182
Gremolata, 78, 84
Grilled Lemon Pepper
Chicken with
Gremolata, 84
Lemon Artichoke
Hearts, 106
Lemon, Lime and
Blueberry Squares, 195
Lemon Rice, 126
Marinated Honey Lemon
Chicken, 87

Lime
Key Lime Pie, 191
Lemon, Lime and
Blueberry Squares, 195
Lime Salad Dressing, 46

Muffins
Best-Ever Blueberry
Muffins, 147
Herta's Favorite Bran
Muffins, 148
Scallion and Goat Cheese
Muffins, 149

Mushrooms
Chicken and Artichoke
Pizzas, 91
Low Country Shrimp and
Grits, 160
Mushroom Squares, 16
Roasted Vegetable
Strata, 153
Ro-Tel Chicken Pasta, 89

Tender Chicken Osker, 88
Veal Scaloppine with
Mushrooms and
Capers, 77

Onions
Onion-Crusted
Salmon, 95
Rosemary Focaccia, 140
South Georgia Baked
Onions, 111
Sweet Vidalia Onion
Scallop, 112

Oranges
Citrus Icing, 182
Citrus Poppy Seed
Delight, 182
Cornucopia Salad, 49
Ginger-Crusted Grouper
with Orange Jalapeño
Sauce, 94
Hot Pepper and Orange
Preserves, 130
Orange Bread, 146
Orange French Toast, 152
Orange Rice, 126

Pasta
Countertop Pasta Sauce
with Brie, 80
Easy Vegetarian Pasta
Sauce, 80
Fifteen-Minute Grilled
Salmon with Angel
Hair, 95
Grandma's Chicken
Noodle Soup, 38
Greek Pasta Salad, 59
Hot Macaroni Salad, 60
Perfect Marinara
Sauce, 81
Ro-Tel Chicken Pasta, 89
Shrimp and Feta Cheese
with Vermicelli, 103
Tortellini Salad, 58

Veal Scaloppine with
Mushrooms and
Capers, 77

Peaches
Peaches and Cream
Crisp, 179
Peaches aux Vin, 180

Peanut Butter
A Little Bit of Everything
Cookies, 197
Asian Grilled Chicken
Salad, 46
Famous Grilled PBJs, 20
Georgia's Evil, 196
Peanut Jade
Marinade, 133
Puppy Chow, 203

Pears
Mixed Greens with Pears
and Gorgonzola, 51
Pears on Pumpernickel, 17

Pies
Buttermilk Pie, 187
Chocolate Icebox Pie, 188
Creamy Blackberry
Pie, 186
Grasshopper Pie, 190
Grits Rum Pie, 193
Heavenly Hash Pie, 192
Ice Cream Pie, 189
Key Lime Pie, 191
Oreo Cookie Coffee Ice
Cream Pie, 188

Pineapple
Blueberry Nut Crunch, 171
Grand Marnier
Pineapple, 178
Heavenly Hash Pie, 192
Hot Baked Fruit, 128
Muesli, 162
Triple-Fruit Salsa, 129

Pizzas
Chicken and Artichoke
Pizzas, 91
Vacation Pizza, 99

Pork. See also Bacon; Ham;
Sausage
Championship Chili, 40
Old-Fashioned Brunswick
Stew, 36
Pork Tenderloin with
Apricot Sauce, 70
Spicy Slow-Cooker
Pork, 71
Tipsy Pork Tenderloin
with Mustard
Sauce, 69

Potatoes
Roasted Sweet
Potatoes, 114
Roasted Vegetables, 123
Arcadian Springs Potato
Salad, 56
Authentic German Potato
Salad, 57
Fish and Potato
Casserole, 96
Garlicky Fried Potato
Spears, 124
Rainy Day Corn
Chowder, 41
Red Potatoes with Vinegar
and Sea Salt, 113
Summer Squash Casserole
in Potato Crust, 116
Vegetables in a
Pouch, 125

Poultry. See Chicken; Turkey

Raspberries
Grand Marnier
Pineapple, 178
Shrimp and Green Bean
Salad, 45

Rice
Black Bean and Rice
Salad, 53
Lemon Rice, 126
Orange Rice, 126
Osso Buco, 78
Sausage and Wild Rice
Casserole, 158
Señor's Mexican Rice, 127
Shortcut Shrimp Creole
with Cheese Rice, 100
Veal Scaloppine with
Mushrooms and
Capers, 77

Salad Dressings
Buck Creek Dressing, 50
Caesar Salad Dressing, 61
Lime Salad Dressing, 46
Oil and Vinegar
Dressing, 49
Poppy Seed Dressing, 61
Red Wine Vinaigrette, 51

Salads
Arcadian Springs Potato
Salad, 56
Asian Grilled Chicken
Salad, 46
Authentic German Potato
Salad, 57
Black Bean and Rice
Salad, 53
Buck Creek Salad, 50
Cornucopia Salad, 49
Greek Pasta Salad, 59
Green Bean Salad, 54
Hot Macaroni Salad, 60
Lakemont Provisions'
Shrimp and Corn
Salad, 44
Layered Cobb Salad, 48
Layered Southwestern
Salad, 55
Light Asparagus
Vinaigrette, 53

Mixed Greens with Pears
   and Gorgonzola, 51
Oriental Coleslaw, 54
Shrimp and Green Bean
   Salad, 45
Tarragon Chicken
   Salad, 47
Tortellini Salad, 58
Wedge Salad with Bacon,
   Tomato and Chive
   Dressing, 52

Salmon
Fifteen-Minute Grilled
   Salmon with Angel
   Hair, 95
Lake Rabun Salmon
   Bites, 17
Onion-Crusted Salmon, 95
Salmon Croquettes, 96

Salsas
Saucy Strawberry Salsa, 29
Triple-Fruit Salsa, 129

Sandwiches
Famous Grilled PBJs, 20
Fried Green Tomato
   Sandwiches, 18
Grilled Turkey Burgers, 92
Turkey Mozzarella Rabun
   Picnic Sandwiches, 19

Sauces
Blender Mayonnaise, 137
Chocolate Sauce, 189
Countertop Pasta Sauce
   with Brie, 80
Easy Vegetarian Pasta
   Sauce, 80
From Fish to Veggies
   Sauce, 136
Garlic Sauce or
   Tum-biz-Zaut, 134
No Pots or Pans
   Hollandaise Sauce, 134

Peanut Jade
   Marinade, 133
Perfect Marinara Sauce, 81
Tartar Sauce, 137
The Best Barbecue
   Sauce, 135
Timesaving Brown Roux
   in the Microwave, 132

Sausage
Breakfast Sausage Grits
   Casserole, 159
Chicken and Sausage
   Gumbo, 35
Sausage and Wild Rice
   Casserole, 158
Sausage Pinwheels, 161
Sausage Yum-Yum, 73
Shortcut Shrimp Creole
   with Cheese Rice, 100
Wonderful Meat Loaf, 68

Seafood. *See also* Crab Meat;
   Fish; Shrimp
Scallops in Scotch and
   Cream, 14

Shrimp
Baked Stuffed
   Shrimp, 102
Double-Batch Shrimp
   Florentine, 101
Lakemont Provisions'
   Shrimp and Corn
   Salad, 44
Low Country Shrimp and
   Grits, 160
Sausalito Crab Dip, 27
Seafood Pizza, 23
Shortcut Shrimp Creole
   with Cheese Rice, 100
Shrimp and Feta Cheese
   with Vermicelli, 103
Shrimp and Green Bean
   Salad, 45
Vacation Pizza, 99

Side Dishes
Cheese Grits, 90
Grits, 160
Hot Baked Fruit, 128
Lemon Rice, 126
Orange Rice, 126
Señor's Mexican Rice, 127

Soups
Championship Chili, 40
Chicken and Sausage
   Gumbo, 35
Delicious Pumpkin, Black
   Bean and Turkey
   Soup, 34
Fireside White Chili, 39
Grandma's Chicken
   Noodle Soup, 38
Old-Fashioned Brunswick
   Stew, 36
Picnic Cucumber Dill
   Soup, 42
Rainy Day Corn
   Chowder, 41
Savory Tomato Soup, 42
Ted's Montana Grill
   Tomato Bisque, 43

Spinach
Double-Batch Shrimp
   Florentine, 101
Eggs Florentine, 154
Light Asparagus
   Vinaigrette, 53
Spicy Spinach Dip, 28
Steamed Spinach with
   Roasted Garlic, 115
Stuffed Tomatoes, 119
Turkey Mozzarella
   Rabun Picnic
   Sandwiches, 19
Vacation Pizza, 99

Spreads
Chèvre with Sun-Dried
   Tomatoes and Basil, 21

Harvest Brie, 21
Hearts of Palm Spread, 22
Herbed Cheesecake, 23
Peppered Marinated Goat
    Cheese, 22
Seafood Pizza, 23

Squash
Delicious Pumpkin, Black
    Bean and Turkey
    Soup, 34
Summer Squash with
    a Twist, 117
Zucchini, Squash and
    Tomato Casserole, 121

Strawberries
Saucy Strawberry Salsa, 29
Strawberry Cake, 184
Strawberry Frosting, 184

Sun-Dried Tomatoes
Chèvre with Sun-Dried
    Tomatoes and Basil, 21
Grilled Turkey Burgers, 92
Peppered Marinated Goat
    Cheese, 22
Sun-Dried Tomato Dip, 29

Tilapia
Fish and Potato
    Casserole, 96
Fish Tacos "A Texas
    Thing," 97

Tomatoes. *See also*
    Sun-Dried Tomatoes
BLT Dip, 24
Broccoli Tomato
    Casserole, 108
Cha Cha Cha Black Bean
    Dip, 24
Championship Chili, 40
Chicken Salsa with Cheese
    Grits Soufflé, 90

Countertop Pasta Sauce
    with Brie, 80
Delicious Pumpkin, Black
    Bean and Turkey
    Soup, 34
Easy Vegetarian Pasta
    Sauce, 80
Fish and Potato
    Casserole, 96
Fish Tacos "A Texas
    Thing," 97
Fried Green Tomato
    Sandwiches, 18
Layered Cobb Salad, 48
Layered Southwestern
    Salad, 55
Old-Fashioned Brunswick
    Stew, 36
Osso Buco, 78
Perfect Marinara Sauce, 81
Roasted Vegetables, 123
Roasted Vegetable
    Strata, 153
Ro-Tel Chicken Pasta, 89
Saucy Strawberry Salsa, 29
Sausage Yum-Yum, 73
Savory Tomato Soup, 42
Shrimp and Feta Cheese
    with Vermicelli, 103
Spicy Slow-Cooker Pork, 71
Spicy Spinach Dip, 28
Stuffed Tomatoes, 119
Ted's Montana Grill
    Tomato Bisque, 43
Tomato Basil Bruschetta, 18
Tomato Pie, 118
Turkey Mozzarella
    Rabun Picnic
    Sandwiches, 19
Veal Scaloppine with
    Mushrooms and
    Capers, 77
Wedge Salad with Bacon,
    Tomato and Chive
    Dressing, 52

Zucchini, Squash and
    Tomato Casserole, 121

Turkey
Delicious Pumpkin, Black
    Bean and Turkey
    Soup, 34
Grilled Turkey Burgers, 92
Turkey Mozzarella Rabun
    Picnic Sandwiches, 19

Veal
Osso Buco, 78
Veal Scaloppine with
    Mushrooms and
    Capers, 77
Wonderful Meat Loaf, 68

Vegetables. *See also*
    Artichokes; Beans;
    Broccoli; Cabbage;
    Corn; Cucumbers;
    Mushrooms; Onions;
    Potatoes; Spinach;
    Squash; Tomatoes;
    Zucchini
Light Asparagus
    Vinaigrette, 53
Delicious Pumpkin, Black
    Bean and Turkey
    Soup, 34
Turnip Greens Casserole
    Style, 120

Venison
Venison Roast, 79

Zucchini
Roasted Vegetable
    Strata, 153
Summer Squash Casserole
    in Potato Crust, 116
Zucchini, Squash and
    Tomato Casserole, 121

LAKE RABUN

Dockside Delights

COOKING

THE LAKE RABUN

WAY

Lake Rabun Food and Fun, Inc.
1485 Rucker Circle
Woodstock, Georgia 30188
(770) 442-9065
(706) 782-7560

YOUR ORDER	QTY	TOTAL
Lake Rabun Dockside Delights at $20.00 per book		$
Georgia residents add $1.40 sales tax per book		$
Postage and handling at $3.00 for first book; $1.00 for each additional book; $9.00 for case of 12		$
	TOTAL	$

Please make check payable to Lake Rabun Food and Fun, Inc.

Name

Street Address

City   State   Zip

Telephone

Photocopies will be accepted.